For Ben & Emi
From Diddy.

QUICK ACCESS TO CHINESE HISTORY

LFINE 10
MIAMI

 FOREIGN LANGUAGES PRESS

First Edition 2008

ISBN 978-7-119- 05487- 2

© Foreign Languages Press, Beijing, China, 2008

Published by
Foreign Languages Press
24 Baiwanzhuang Road, Beijing 100037, China
http://www.flp.com.cn

Distributed by
China International Book Trading Corporation
35 Chegongzhuang Xilu, Beijing 100044, China
P. O. Box 399, Beijing, China

Printed in the People's Republic of China

Preface

Since remote antiquity, the winding river of Chinese history has been flowing onward, through time to reach today's banks, and still coursing into the future.

Absorbing countless brooks and streams, surging through obstacles, this great river gave birth to China, one of the most splendid civilizations in the world.

However, the very profoundness and length of this history poses difficulties for readers to explore its myths and treasures. Thus, a book that provides quick access to Chinese history would be a most handy tool for readers.

Our book is such a tool, presenting the major points of Chinese history along a complete timeline, with comparisons between the concurrent histories of China and the rest of the world. Covering a time span from 1,700,000 years ago up to AD 1911, the book includes influential historical events and figures in Chinese history, arranged in chronological order with pictures, illustrations, maps and charts.

Distinguishing this book from other general introductory books on Chinese history, its contents have been arranged along a timeline, with the function of quick access highlighted by its innovative layout and a detailed index. For readers who wish to learn about the history of a specific period, the target contents are at your fingertips, through the clear time indicators at the top of the pages. And for readers who want to look up specific events or figures, the INDEX guides you directly to the information you want. With this book, international readers will be given a clear vision of the major developments in Chinese history and culture.

Contents

Explanatory Notes

1. The book starts with Yuanmou Man (c. 1,700,000 years ago), the first primitive humans in China, and ends with the 1911 Revolution and the fall of the last feudal dynasty in Chinese history.

2. The book has 455 points in Chinese history, covering facts from various dynasties, historical events and figures, important writings, technologies, arts, and political and social systems. The entries selected are those considered most significant and influential in Chinese history.

3. The List of Entries is arranged in alphabetical order, with date and location specified for each entry.

4. The contents of the book are arranged along a complete timeline of Chinese history. Historical events are arranged by their dates, which are marked on the timeline, while the entry titles below the timeline specify their duration. For example, "184" is marked on the timeline as the year when the Yellow Turban Army Uprising started, and "(184-192)" after the title below indicates its duration. Historical figures are placed in the periods corresponding to their activities, without specific dates marked on the timeline, while their years of birth and death can be found in the entries.

5. The book has a special design to introduce the Chinese dynasties. Each dynasty occupies a new page, with a yellowish background and a red timeline (including a seal inscribed with "Chinese History," the years of the dynasty, and subtitle). To highlight the dynasties, a special bold font is used to differentiate them from other historical entries.

6. The book has over 400 pictures related to the entries. Including brief captions, the images serve as illuminating illustrations bringing history to life.

7. The book also has important concurrent world events and figures listed at the bottom of some pages, providing a comparative development of Chinese history and world history.

8. The INDEX is arranged in alphabetical order to provide quick access to names, places, historical events, and glossary.

9. The chronology of Chinese dynasties in the APPENDIX is arranged in time order along a knotted rope, as tribute to the ancient knotting-cord method to record events. The starting and ending years are marked for each dynasty, along with pictures presenting the features of the era.

LIST OF ENTRIES

D

QUICK ACCESS
TO CHINESE HISTORY

c. 1,700,000 years ago

c. 1,000,000 years ago

c. 710,000 - 230,000 years ago

⬤ **Yuanmou Man**   ⬤ **Lantian Man**   ⬤ **Peking Man**

⬤ Yuanmou Man was the first Homo erectus in China. In 1965, two fossil teeth were discovered in Yunnan Province, southwest China, and the owner of the teeth was named "Yuanmou Man" (*Homo erectus Yuanmouensis*). Traces of the use of fire and stone tools were also discovered. As the earliest primitive humans in Asia, Yuanmou Man was the first hominid known to control fire.

Yuanmou Man using fire

Reproduction of Lantian Man

⬤ "Lantian Man" (*Homo erectus lantianensis*) refers to human beings living in the early phase of the Upper Paleolithic period. Remnants of Lantian Man were found in 1963 and 1964 in Lantian County, Shaanxi Province, and included a skull, a mandible, a maxilla, and over 10 teeth. Stone tools and animal fossils were also discovered in the same strata as the Lantian fossils.

⬤ The "Peking Man" (*Homo erectus pekinensis*) refers to the human beings living in northeast China in the Lower Paleolithic period. In 1929, Chinese archeologist Pei Wenzhong discovered a complete skullcap at Dragon Bone Hill, Zhoukoudian, Beijing. Later, traces of the use of fire and stone tools were also discovered.

Reproduction of Peking Man

4.16.10

c. 80,000 - 10,000 years ago

5000 - 4000 BC

- Upper Cave Man
- Paddy rice cultivation
- The emergence of lacquerware

Animal bone needles and teeth beads made by Upper Cave Man

● The "Upper Cave Man" refers to human beings living in northeast China during the Upper Paleolithic period. At the excavation site of Dragon Bone Hill, Zhoukoudian, Beijing, archeologists found three skulls and other human fossils of at least eight hominids, a large number of animal fossils, along with carbon dust, stone tools, bone tools, and jewelry made of beaded stones, animal teeth and shells.

Paddy rice from Hemudu Culture site

● Along the lower reaches of the Yangtze River, Zhejiang Province, archeologists at the Hemudu Culture sites discovered numerous remains of rice and cultivating tools (spades made from animal shoulder bones). Evidence of rice cultivation was also found.

Spades made from animal shoulder bones and other bone tools from Hemudu Culture site

● Lacquerware craft refers to the application of lacquer sap to the surface of wooden furnishings. With lacquer sealant, implements became rot and water resistant, and easier to be painted on. In 1978, archeologists at the Hemudu Culture site excavated a wooden bowl coated with a thin layer of red lacquer.

Red-lacquered wooden bowl from Hemudu Culture site

4800 - 2900 BC   4300 - 2500 BC

▶ Origin of pottery

Pottery basin painted with
a human face and fish

▶ From the remains of the Yangshao Culture of this period in northeast and northwest China, archeologists have discovered numerous exquisite pottery products. These potteries are mainly red in color, often with geometric patterns or animal-shaped designs, indicating people then had mastered pottery-making techniques such as clay selecting, shaping, decorating, firing, and other processes.

Pottery-making by stacking
clay coils

▶ The Dawenkou Culture

▶ The Dawenkou Culture sites are mainly located in Shandong and northern Jiangsu provinces. Dawenkou communities lived mainly by grain cultivation, as well as hunting, fishing and picking wild edibles. The tools used include hatchets, shovels, knives, hoes made of bone, fishing darts and hooks, among others. Pottery wheels began to be used to produce more delicate and diversified vessels. The symbols inscribed in the vessels resemble pictographs, referred to by archeologists as "Pottery Inscriptions."

Painted pottery vessel

▶ The emergence of early acupuncture

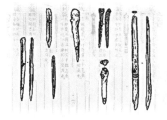

Primitive bone needles used for
acupuncture

▶ The earliest forms of acupuncture used stone needles or chips to prick acupuncture points on the human body, with the purpose of easing pain and curing illnesses by stimulating the regulatory functions of the nervous system. Later, stone needles were replaced by metal needles, and a complete set of treatment methods was developed. Acupuncture occupies a very important position in Traditional Chinese Medicine (TCM), and is very effective in treating neurological and dysfunctional ailments.

○ 5000-4000 BC: A calendar based on the movement of the sun and the moon appeared in Egypt, regarded as the first calendar of humankind.

4000 - 3000 BC

3300 BC

Hongshan Culture

The Majiayao Culture (3300 - 2900 BC)

Painted pottery vessel

Located mainly in Inner Mongolia and western Liaoning Province, Hongshan Culture was a good example of Neolithic culture in northern China. The community lived on agricultural production, animal husbandry (keeping livestock such as pigs, cattle, and sheep), as well as fishing. The production tools found varied in materials. The stone artifacts included simply struck tools, abraded tools, and finely made tools. Potteries were either finely painted vessels or crude containers with simple patterns. The people had also developed fine techniques of jade carving. Among the many jade artifacts, a C-shaped jade dragon excavated in Chifeng, Inner Mongolia, best represents the culture's jade carving craft. Elegantly coiled in a "C," the jade dragon vibrantly features a rising mouth and flowing hair.

C-shaped jade dragon

Pottery basin painted with dancing figures

From the Late Neolithic period, the Majiayao Culture sites are mainly located in the upper reaches of the Yellow River and the Tao, Daxia and Huangshui river valleys in today's Gansu and Qinghai provinces. Following the Yangshao Culture in central China, the Majiayao Culture brought painted pottery culture to unprecedented levels. The pottery vessels unearthed are highly varied in shape, design and color, with fantastic animal designs, magnificent images of singing and dancing, contrasting geometric patterns, and dynamic postures. Not only bearing mysterious social and cultural data on the prehistoric period, the pottery also reveals the earliest form of Chinese painting — using the paint brush as a tool, lines for modeling, and black (Chinese ink) as a basic tone.

Pottery urn decorated with human-figures relief

◎ 3500-3100 BC: The emergence of pottery wheels in Mesopotamia, and the invention of cuneiform scripts.

◎ 3500-3100 BC: The formation of ancient Egyptian states and the appearance of hieroglyphs.

The Liangzhu Culture (3300 - 2200 BC)

The Yellow Emperor and the Yan Emperor

Portrait of the
Yellow Emperor

Decorative jade mask

Liangzhu was a Neolithic culture in the lower reaches of the Yangtze River, with sites mainly located around Lake Tai. It featured black pottery with thin-walled bodies and polished surfaces. A small number of pottery vessels were carved with delicate designs and hollowed-out holes. The finest potteries of the Liangzhu Culture include three-legged pots (*ding*) with fine bird and dragon designs, and vessels with lacquer coating. Jade articles were highly developed, in the forms of beads and tubes. Along with deity-beast motifs, the most frequent images are of birds.

The legendary Yellow Emperor is venerated by Chinese people as the "ancestor of humanity." Legend has it that, the reign of the Yellow Emperor witnessed the inventions of sericulture, land and water transportation, written Chinese characters, music, medicine, mathematics and calendars, among other things. The Yan Emperor was another legendary figure from the same period, said to have been defeated by the Yellow Emperor. The latter then unified all the tribes to form the "Huaxia Clan." Therefore, the Yellow Emperor and the Yan Emperor are both revered as the common ancestors of the Chinese nation, and Chinese people today still call themselves the "descendants of the Yellow Emperor and the Yan Emperor."

Portrait of the
Yan Emperor

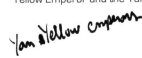

Clay *ding*
(three-legged pot)

2600 - 2000 BC

● **Sericulture and silk reeling**
● **Cangjie, the inventor of Chinese writing**

● **The Longshan Culture**

● Legend has it that Leizu, the wife of the Yellow Emperor (see "Yellow Emperor and Yan Emperor"), discovered that silkworms could form cocoons to produce silk. So she began planting mulberry trees, raising silkworms and boiling cocoons. Since then, raising silkworms, reeling silk and producing silk fabrics gradually developed to become one of the major industries of Chinese working people, while silk fabrics became a major product for trading. The technology of silk fabric production began to spread all over the world during the 3rd and 4th centuries.

Black pottery wine vessel

● The Longshan Culture refers to the relics of the central and lower reaches of the Yellow River from the Late Neolithic period. The sites are mainly located in Shandong, Henan, Shanxi and Shaanxi provinces. City remains and black pottery distinguish the Longshan Culture. Dawenkou Culture techniques of pottery wheels were generally adopted in this period, producing quantities of polished black pottery of finer quality. Pottery vessels with eggshell-thin walls were produced, with surfaces polished to a degree as if lacquered. This period is regarded as an apex in Chinese pottery-making history.

Portrait of Cangjie

● In primeval times, people mainly used the "rope knot tying" method to record events. Legend has it that Cangjie, official historian of the Yellow Emperor, invented different symbols by observing the distribution of the constellations, the patterns of mountain ranges and rivers, the prints of insects, fish, birds and animals, and the shapes of grasses, leaves and trees, as well as various vessels and implements. Then he attached a meaning to each symbol. This is believed in Chinese folklore to mark the beginning of Chinese characters as pictographs.

Delicate black pottery goblet

○ 2780-2280 BC: In ancient Egyptian areas, the unification of nations was completed, an autocratic monarchy established, and large-scale pyramid construction began.

● **The Qijia Culture**

● **Da Yu's flood control (c. 2235 - 2213 BC)**

● The Qijia Culture was mainly distributed around the upper Yellow River region of Gansu and Qinghai provinces, and its tributaries northwest of Shaanxi Province, western Inner Mongolia and parts of Ningxia. As a transitional culture between the Stone and Bronze ages, the Qijia Culture had three major

Double-handled red clay vessel

features: first, pottery vessels with unique features; second, emerging copperware and bronzeware; third, unique jade vessels. The jade vessels were especially rich in variety and refined in quality. Hotan jade began to be used for making ritual implements such as *cong* (square column-shaped container), *bi* (flat disk with center circular hole), *huan* (ring), *huang* (curved bow-shaped), *yue* (crescent-shaped axe), *dao* (sword), and *zhang* (tablet).

Jade *cong* (square container with circular interior)

● In the 23rd century BC, China's Yellow River regularly flooded, and the legendary Emperor Shun appointed Yu to control the floods. Yu employed principles of channeling and dredging, and after 13 years of effort, 9 rivers were channeled so the floods flowed to the sea. "Yu the Great" was so successful that Emperor Shun transferred his power to him.

Da Yu

Da Yu controlling floods

◎ *c.* 2300-1750 BC: During the times of the Harappan Culture in ancient India, cities emerged and nations formed. Written scripts were used.

2070 - 1600 BC

The Xia Dynasty

As the first dynasty in China's recorded history, the Xia Dynasty governed areas along the Yellow River. During the 400-year reign of the dynasty, only the sixth ruler brought this country some prosperity. The other 15 kings were all helpless in the face of internal power struggles and external tribal invasions. Eventually, the Xia Dynasty ended in the hands of the last ruler, Jie, corrupted through a life of luxury, dissipation and arrogance. The one who ended the Xia Dynasty was named Tang, establishing a new empire — the Shang Dynasty.

The power transfer system and hereditary system

The tribal societies of China adopted a power transfer system, in which the ruler voluntarily abdicated and selected a wise man to succeed him and manage tribal affairs. The three famous tribal leaders in the Yellow River region, Yao, Shun and Yu accomplished power transfer in this way. Upon Yu's death, his son Qi proclaimed himself the king, marking the replacement of the old power transfer system by a hereditary system. The first nation in Chinese history, the Xia Dynasty, was thus established.

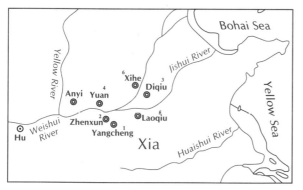

Xia Dynasty's territory and shifting of its capital

A Xia-dynasty excavation site at Erlitou, Yanshi, Henan Province

◎ c. 2100 BC: Ur-Nammu, the founder of the 3rd Dynasty of Ur (Ur III), established the world's earliest law codes, the *Code of Ur-Nammu*.

◎ 2100-1400 BC: The period of Cretan Culture in the Aegean Sea region.

c. 2000 BC

The Lunar Calendar

Also called the "Xia (Summer) Calendar," the Lunar Calendar is said to have originated in 2000 BC, and developed over the following several thousand years. In this calendar, there are 12 months in a year, 29 or 30 days in a month, and altogether 354 or 355 days in a year. The calendar eventually also designated a "Leap Month" to make up a tropical year. It determined 24 seasonal division points to reflect the changing features of seasons. The Lunar Calendar had an enormous influence on Chinese history, and Chinese people around the world still use it to guide agricultural production, and to mark traditional festivals such as the Spring Festival, the Mid-Autumn and Dragon-boat festivals, etc.

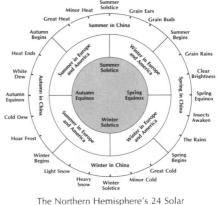

The Northern Hemisphere's 24 Solar Terms and 4 Seasons

The Ganzhi Dating System

Ganzhi was a unique dating system in ancient China. "Ganzhi" is an abbreviation, of the second characters of Tiangan and Dizhi. Tiangan (Heavenly Stems) had 10 stems, while Dizhi (Earthly Branches) comprised 12 branches. The combination of the Tiangan stems and the Dizhi branches gives 60 exhaustive possibilities, forming a sexagesimal dating system. A dating system using Tiangan first came into use in the Xia Dynasty, and the combined Ganzhi system appeared in the Shang Dynasty. An exact Ganzhi dating system first appeared in the third year of the reign of Duke Yin of Lu (720 BC) in the Spring and Autumn Period, and continued in use for the following 2,600 years, without any disruption, until AD 1911. The Ganzhi Dating System is regarded as the world's oldest and most complete known dating system.

◎ 2000 BC: The Phonicians invented the Phoenician alphabet.
◎ 2000-1000 BC: The Vedic Period in early stages of ancient India.
◎ 1900-1650 BC: The Old Hittite Kingdom in ancient west Asia.
◎ c. 1894-1595 BC: Ancient Babylon in Mesopotamia.

1600 - 1046 BC

The Shang Dynasty

With 31 kings reigning for over 500 years, the Shang Dynasty had once expanded its territory from the Yellow River to the Yangtze River, with many vassal states. The Shang kings carried out the "Cooperative Farming System," and enhanced the circulation of commodities across the country. Written characters for communal use gradually came into form, while exquisite techniques developed in architecture, lacquer vessels, bone sculpture, bronzeware, and other fields.

Square wide-mouth bronze vessel with four ram heads

The royal hunting expeditions

The kings of the Shang Dynasty often led aristocrats and armies on large-scale hunting expeditions. These well-organized expeditions helped train the army and obtain sufficient food for the court, and more importantly, kept the nobility loyal to the kings. The practice of royal hunting expeditions lasted until the mid-18th century.

Bronze tetrapod decorated with animal-patterned studs

Oxen bones recording Shang Dynasty hunting expeditions

◎ 1792-1750 BC: In ancient Babylon, King Hammurabi enacted a set of laws called the *Code of Hammurabi*, the first written code of laws in human history.

◎ *c.* 1700-1100 BC: The Mycenaean Civilization in the Aegean.

Sanxingdui Culture

Sanxingdui, located in Guanghan, Sichuan Province, is a relic site of the Bronze Age in southwest China. The uncovered ruins of a city, 1,600-2,100m long from east to west and 1,400m wide from north to south, totaled an area of 26,000 sq km. Two large sacrificial pits were found near the ancient city ruins, and over 4,000 gold, bronze and jade artifacts were unearthed. Among these artifacts, the most mysterious was a 2.62-meter-high bronze statue, along with over 50 giant bronze sculpted heads with protruding eyes, some of them wearing metal masks. The Sanxingdui Culture bears strong Shang-dynasty characteristics, and also reflects the importance of religion and sorcery in ancient Sichuan culture.

Gold-gilded bronze human head sculpture

Giant human mask

King Pangeng moved the Shang capital to Yin

The capital of the Shang was moved for many times during the first 300 years of the dynasty. The constant change of the capital city did not stop until the 20th king, Pangeng, finally moved the capital to Yin, now to the northwest of Anyang, Henan Province. The new capital Yin developed into a dynamic large city, bringing unprecedented prosperity to the country. Today, evidence of past prosperity can still be seen at the Ruins of Yin.

Shang-dynasty wine vessel from the Yin Ruins

Clay drainpipes from the Yin Ruins

© 1584-1071 BC: The New Kingdom period of ancient Egypt.
© 1430-1200 BC: The Hittite Empire in Anatolia (Asia Minor).

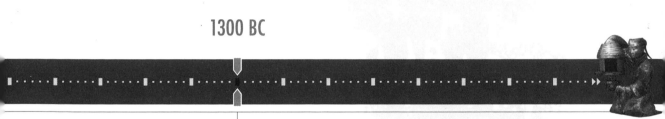

Oracle-Bone Script

Huanhe River in Anyang, Henan Province

Zaifeng Oracle Bone, recording imperial remuneration on one side, with decorative designs on the other

At the beginning of the 20th century, archeologists found nearly 100,000 turtle shells and animal bones in the Ruins of Yin, capital of the Shang Dynasty. The approximately 5,000 different pictographs carved on these oracle bones recorded the relationship between divinations and political activities in the Shang, as well as contents of sacrifices, military operations, official appointments, city construction, good or bad omens for the country, etc. Oracle-bone script was the earliest known Chinese writing.

Ox bone recording Shang Dynasty social life

◎ 1400 – 1078 BC: The Old Assyrian Period in ancient West Asia.

◎ 1379 BC: Upon succession to the throne, Pharaoh Akhenaten (r. 1379-1362 BC) undertook religious reforms and compelled monotheistic worship of Aten (Sun God).

c. 1200 BC　　　　　　　1075 BC

The Simuwu Tetrapod

King Zhou of Shang
(r. 1075 - 1046 BC)

King Wen of Zhou

The Simuwu Tetrapod is a typical Shang bronze vessel of high technical competence. As a ritual vessel used in the middle of the dynasty, the Simuwu Tetrapod is 975 kg in weight, 133 cm in height, and was made from an alloy of copper, tin and lead. Its name comes from the three Chinese characters "*si mu wu*" inscribed on the inner walls. It is a rectangular vessel with four hollow legs and two vertical loop handles. There are decorative patterns all over the vessel, except on the centers of the four faces.

King Zhou (posthumous name), the last king of the Shang Dynasty, was a tyrant. He preferred drinking and other pleasures to proper governance, ignoring almost all affairs of state. Government officials who tried to persuade him were often severely punished or killed. In the end, King Zhou was utterly isolated, and overthrown by a tribal clan with the name "Zhou."

Portrait of King Wen
of Zhou

King Wen of Zhou (1152-1056 BC), named Ji Chang, was a leader of the Zhou clan in the late Shang Dynasty. Under his honorable rule, the Zhou state gradually grew in power. Seeing the Shang Dynasty on the brink of collapse, the vassal states shifted allegiance to Ji Chang. However, Ji never proclaimed himself king. It was his son, King Wu of Zhou, who ended the Shang Dynasty and established the Zhou Dynasty. Ji Chang was henceforth honored as King Wen of Zhou.

Simuwu Tetrapod

◎ 1100-700 BC: Homer in the Hellenistic period of ancient Greece.

1046 - 771 BC

The Battle of Muye

● The Zhou Dynasty located its capital at Haojing (now southwest Xi'an, Shaanxi). The 275 years that followed marked the reign of the Western Zhou in Chinese history. During this period, the administrative systems of the country were

Portrait of King Wu of Zhou

basically formulated. The adoption of the patriarchal clan and enfeoffment systems greatly strengthened central control over local governments, and overall territory far surpassed that of the Shang Dynasty. However, none of the Western Zhou kings could eradicate the threats from the tribal clans, and the dynasty was ultimately ended by the Quanrong nomadic tribe from the far northwest.

● The people known as the Zhou were a tribe living in the Yellow River region. Under the leadership of King Wen and King Wu, the Zhou gradually became powerful. In 1045 BC, King Wu (r. 1049-1043 BC) led a military expedition against the capital of Shang, and the two parties engaged in a fierce battle at Muye (south of present-day Qixian County, Henan). Many Shang soldiers changed sides and joined the Zhou army, to end the brutal reign of their king. King Zhou fled to his palace, where he burned himself to death. Then King Wu proclaimed the Zhou Dynasty.

Gui (cup with two handles), food container in the Western Zhou, recording King Wu's campaign against the Shang

◎ 1000 BC: The Hebrews established the Kingdom of Judah, with the capital as Jerusalem. The kingdom ended in 586 BC.

The patriarchal clan and the enfeoffment systems

The patriarchal clan and enfeoffment systems constituted the hierarchical structure of the Western Zhou that governed tribal, religious, political and military affairs of the country. The King of Zhou was the supreme ruler, and only his legitimate sons could inherit the throne, with the right to perform rituals. Principalities given by the king to members of the royal family constituted the sovereign foundation. Lords of the principalities had obligations to provide soldiers and chariots during wars. Reign through consanguinity dominated all social and political structures in the Western Zhou. However, with the increasing power of vassal states and imbalanced development of principalities, the system's defects were gradually exposed in the late Western Zhou. Frequent battles were fought between the vassal states, and even the king was controlled by a certain vassal to command others. This chaotic period continued until mid-3rd century BC.

The Well-field System in Western Zhou

The well-field farming system was carried out in the Western Zhou. In this system, a tract of land was divided into nine squares, like the Chinese character 井 (jing or well), with the grain from the middle square taken by the government and that of surrounding squares kept by individual farmers after paying tax. Because "all lands belonged to the king," cultivated land could not be sold or transferred, but was inherited by family members.

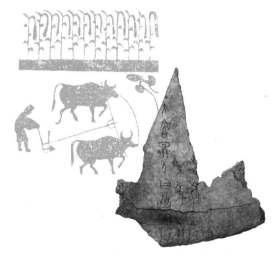

Ox bone recording tilling of farmland

I Ching (Book of Changes)

The book *Yi*, also called *I Ching*, was first composed in the 11th century BC, and then further supplemented and interpreted. It is a very ancient book on prediction and divination in China. The book is composed of two parts: the Ching (text) and the Zhuan (explanations of the Ching). The Ching is mainly about the 64 hexagrams (64 Gua) and the six-stacked horizontal lines (Yao) of which the hexagrams are composed. There is a text for each of the hexagrams and lines. The Zhuan explains the meanings of the texts, as well as the origin and nature of the eight trigrams (combinations of hexagrams and lines). Because of its profound and mystical meanings, countless interpretations and explanations have been offered in the past several thousand years. *I Ching* is revered by Confucianism and Taoism as an important classic, and has also been widely studied around the world.

Bronze bell sets, ritual implements and ritual music

Bianzhong (bronze bell set) and *bianqing* (stone chimes) were ancient musical instruments in China, and the *ding* was a food container as well as a ritual vessel. Though these three items had emerged long before, hierarchical and political significance was not attached to them until the Western Zhou. *Bianzhong* was made from bronze, and *bianqing* from stone or jade. They were hung in melodic sequence on a wooden frame and struck with a mallet. *Ding* were generally food vessels made from bronze. The bells and chimes were struck for their melody and a set of *ding* was arrayed on important occasions such as receiving foreign envoys, performing sacrificial rituals, and holding feasts. However, the melody and number of *ding* varied according to a strict set of hierarchical regulations.

Bronze bell set from the Tomb of
Marquis Yi of Zeng in Hubei Province

◎ 935 - 612 BC: During the Neo-Assyrian Empire period in ancient West Asia, ironware appeared and became widely used.

◎ *c.* 10th-5th centuries BC: The *Upanishads*, the earliest philosophical writings of ancient India were composed.

The Gonghe Regency

The first recorded earthquake

King You fooled nobles with beacons

The 9th century BC saw the strengthening power of minor nobility and civilians who could not officially participate in politics, challenging the absolute reign of the Zhou royal nobility. In 841 BC, minor nobles who called themselves "countrymen" revolted, and forced King Li out of the capital city. The 14-year Gonghe Regency started, under the co-leadership of Duke of Shao and Duke of Zhou. This is the beginning of date-recording in Chinese history.

Facsimile of Bamboo Annals

Earthquakes were long recorded by the ancient Chinese. *Bamboo Annals* (ancient historical writing) kept a simple record of the earthquake on Mount Tai in 1831 BC. Later, *Shi Jing* (Book of Odes) described in detail a major earthquake, in what is now the Shaanxi area, in 780 BC. They are generally regarded as the earliest recorded earthquake in China and around the world.

The last king of Western Zhou, King You, ordered the beacons (emergency military signal) be lighted in order to win a smile from Baosi, his beloved concubine. When the nobility hurriedly arrived with troops, they saw nothing but a sweet smile from Baosi. They left extremely angry. Then in 770 BC, when the Quanrong nomadic tribe from the northwest forced its way toward the capital, King Zhou had the beacons lit again, but none of the nobility came to his rescue. And thus the Western Zhou ended.

◎ 850 BC: The Phoenicians established the Carthaginian Empire, which ended in 146 BC.

◎ 800-550 BC: The Post-Vedic Period of ancient India.

◎ 776 BC: The Greeks held a series of athletic competitions in Olympia in honor of Zeus, marking the beginning of the Olympic Games.

770 - 256 BC

The Eastern Zhou Dynasty ● The Spring and Autumn Period (770 - 476 BC)

● After the collapse of the Western Zhou, the Zhou royal family moved eastwards to a new capital, Luoyi (now Luoyang, Henan), which is referred to in Chinese history as the "Eastern Zhou." With the scope of reign sizably shrunken and central power greatly weakened, the king of Eastern Zhou was no more than a nominal political figurehead. The vassal states were engaged in battles against each other, basically ignoring the king. The Eastern Zhou survived the Spring and Autumn and the Warring States periods, and was finally ended by the Qin in 256 BC.

Alliance treaties from the
Spring and Autumn Period

● By the 5th century BC, the Eastern Zhou had declined, and the vassal states continued on their own paths of development. In the Yellow River region, the states of Qi, Lu, Jin, Song and Qin fought for supremacy, while the states of Chu, Wu and Yue in the Yangtze River region gradually gained power. These states became influential, though the King of Zhou was still viewed as the nominal supreme ruler. This chaotic time was called the "Spring and Autumn Period."

◎ 8th century BC: The legendary poet Homer composed the ancient Greek epics *Iliad* and *Odyssey*.

◎ 753- 509 BC: The Roman Kingdom period with a monarchical government.

Guan Zhong and his reforms

Five Powers of the Spring and Autumn Period

Records of comet sightings

Portrait of Guanzhong

Guan Zhong (725-645 BC) was an eminent statesman in the State of Qi during the Spring and Autumn Period. He carried out multiple civil, economic and political reforms and made his country the first hegemony in central China. The contents of the reforms were: first, collecting taxes according to the quality of farming lands, and imposing state monopolies on salt, iron and mintage, to strengthen the country's economy; second, dividing the capital city into yeomen and trade villages, the countryside into five subdivisions, and appointing administrators for each; third, further changing yeomen villages into military formations to prepare for war, and expanding armaments.

During the Spring and Autumn Period, several larger states arose out of the 140 vassal states, after years of warfare and annexation. In their contention for supremacy, these powerful states launched for many years countless campaigns against each other. In 679 BC, with the assistance of Guan Zhong, Duke Huan of Qi was the first to gain supremacy among the states, but later was replaced one after another by Duke Wen of Jin, King Zhuang of Chu, King Helü of Wu, and King Goujian of Yue. They were collectively known as the Five Powers of the Spring and Autumn Period.

The Power Restoration of Duke Wen of Jin (detail)

Records of comet sightings during the Western Han

China was the first country to keep records of sightings of comets. In *Spring and Autumn Annals*, a brief record of a periodic comet in 613 BC is noted: "In the 7th lunar month, a comet shot towards the Great Dipper." In *Records of the Historian*, a detailed record of a periodic comet was noted in 240 BC: "In the 7th year of the First Emperor of Qin, a comet was seen in the east, then in the north, and in the west in the 5th lunar month... and was seen in the west again 16 days later."

◎ 660 BC: The reign of Emperor Jimmu, the first emperor of Japan, began.
◎ 626-538 BC: The Neo-Babylonian Empire in Mesopotamia.
◎ Late 7th century BC: Spartan state formed in ancient Greece.

The Iron Age

Schools of thoughts flourished

Chushuimu tax system

Chinese people began smelting iron in the early phase of the Spring and Autumn Period, which became a common practice by the end of the period. Iron weapons, farming tools and vessels were excavated from tombs in the Yellow and Yangtze river regions. In 513 BC, an iron *ding* (vessel), inscribed with a criminal law code, was cast in the State of Jin. In the Warring States Period, blast cupola furnaces were used for smelting iron. The iron-smelting industry was monopolized by the state, and the officials in charge administered a large number of subordinates to exploit mines and smelt iron. Iron farming tools played a vital role in agriculture, while iron weapons served as the key to success in battles.

Copper-handled iron sword from the Spring and Autumn Period

During the approximately 400-year period starting from 7th century BC, China experienced continuing chaos. Yet it was also an era of great cultural and intellectual expansion, with many schools of thought flourishing. Confucianism, Legalism and Taoism were founded in this period, and other schools of thought such as Mohism and the Yin-Yang School (of Naturalists) also started in this era. For over 2,000 years, these schools of thought exerted profound and far-reaching influence on the development of Chinese society and the thinking of the Chinese people.

In 594 BC, the agricultural taxation system, "Chushuimu," was imposed according to the size of farming lands in the State of Lu. It was stipulated that landowners pay taxes according to the size of their cultivated lands, with a 10% rate. This event marked the beginning of private ownership of lands and agricultural tax in ancient China.

○ 621 BC: Draconic Constitution was enacted in ancient Athens.

○ 597-538 BC: Babylonian Captivity, the deportation and exile of Jews of the ancient Kingdom of Judah to Babylon.

○ 594 BC: As statesman of Athens, Solon (638-559 BC) started the civil conference and jury system, marking the beginning of civilian participation. in political affairs and the establishment of a jury in judicial courts.

● Laozi and *Daodejing*

Laozi

● Laozi (*c.* 580-500 BC), named Li Er, lived in the State of Chu in the late Spring and Autumn Period. As the founder of Daoism (Taoism), he left a great legacy to Chinese philosophers with *Daodejing* (*The Book of the Way and Virtue*), one of the most significant treatises in Chinese cosmogony. The book illustrated the origin and evolution of all creatures in the universe through the concept of *Dao* (the Way or the Path). "Out of *Dao*, One is born; Out of One, Two; Out of Two, Three; Out of Three, the created universe." "*Dao* models itself after nature." The book also talks of the unity of opposites, arguing that two opposing sides transform into each other, as in, "Disaster is an avenue for fortune, (and) fortune is concealment for disaster." A governing approach resembling laissez-faire was encouraged for rulers.

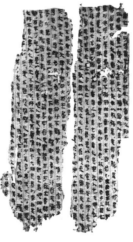

Daodejing (*The Book of the Way and Virtue*) on silk

● Confucius

Confucius

● Born in the State of Lu, Confucius (Kong Qiu or Kongzi, 551-479 BC) was the great thinker and educator of ancient China. As the founder of Confucianism, he valued *ren* (benevolence/goodness) and *li* (etiquette/ritual) as the highest ethical principles to guide people's conduct. Confucius started private teaching of students, and accepted disciples regardless of their origins. It is said that he had 3,000 disciples,

◎ The ancient Greek philosopher Thales (624-547 BC) founded the Milesian school of thought.

◎ The philosopher Anaximander (611-545 BC) composed *On Nature*, the first philosophical classic of ancient Greece.

Book of Odes

with 72 of them outstanding. In education, he proposed: "The student, having completed his learning, should apply himself to become an official"; and "to teach students in accordance with their aptitude." More famed quotes include: "As I walk alongside others, they may serve as my teachers"; "Be not ashamed to ask and learn from inferiors"; and "To know what you know, and know what you do not — that is 'knowledge'." The words of Confucius were recorded by his disciples in *Confucian Analects*. Confucius traveled to various states to promulgate his thinking, yet often met with failure. In his old age, he devoted himself to studying ancient literature, and compiled *Shi Jing* (*Book of Odes*), *Shangshu* (*Classic of History*), and *Chunqiu* (*Spring and Autumn Annals*). As guiding philosophical principles, Confucianism has exerted great influence on the Chinese people for over 2,000 years.

Facsimile of *Shi Jing* (*Book of Odes*)

Collecting August Dates, by Qing artist Wu Qiu, according to the contents of *Guo Feng* (*State Winds*) in *Shi Jing* (*Book of Odes*)

● *Book of Odes*, the earliest collection of Chinese poems and odes, was compiled and edited by Confucius. It comprises 305 folksongs and festive songs, dating from the Western Zhou Dynasty to the mid Spring and Autumn Period. The collection is divided into three parts according to genre, namely *feng*, *ya*, and *song*. *Feng* were mainly folksongs (airs) from vassal states in the Yellow River region. The *ya* genre was festive songs sung in the Zhou court. And *song* contained hymns and eulogies sung at sacrificial rites to deities and ancestral spirits of the Zhou royal house. These odes recounted Zhou life in various aspects: religious observances, sacrificial rituals, agricultural production, feasts and banquets, political policies, warfare and compulsory labor, as well as romance and marriage. Exalted as one of the most important Confucian classics, *Book of Odes* exerted unfailing influence on later poets in selection of themes, structure, and language use.

◎ Sakyamuni (Gautama Buddha, 565-483 BC) founded comprehensive Buddhist doctrines.

◎ Pythagoras (*c*.580-500 BC), an ancient Greek mathematician and philosopher, founded Pythagoreanism, proposed the Pythagorean theorem, including the theory of the transmigration of souls, and that numbers constitute the true nature of things.

Deng Xi

Sun Wu and *The Art of War*

Lu Ban

Living in the State of Zheng at the end of the Spring and Autumn Period, Deng Xi (545-501 BC) was once a court official. He opened a private school, and formulated the Criminal Law Codes on bamboo slips to publicize the idea of ruling through law. He was noted for his eloquence, for being "ambiguous in wording and inexhaustible in language." Actively engaged in early legal work, Deng Xi had a great impact on later lawyers. He could be considered the first lawyer in China, and the originator of the profession.

Portrait of Sun Wu

Composed by Sun Wu, a military strategist in the late Spring and Autumn Period, *The Art of War* comprised 13 chapters, summaries on the experience of battles fought between states, as well as basic principles of strategies and tactics. The book touched upon various military aspects, including planning and calculations, waging war, strategic attacks, key factors in war, strategies and tactics, scouting and spying. Based on practices of warfare in a turbulent era, *The Art of War* was not only extensively studied and used in the Spring and Autumn Period, but also came to be regarded as prerequisite by later military officers and theorists around the world.

From the State of Lu in the late Spring and Autumn Period, Gongshu Ban (507-444 BC) was later known as "Lu Ban." Born to a craftsman family, Lu Ban produced many inventions including: the saw, plane, drill and chisel used by carpenters; the "cloud ladder," a mobile counterweighted siege ladder used in wars, as well as the grappling hook and ram, and naval warfare implements; a bamboo and wood bird as a proto-kite; and a wooden horse carriage. He was acknowledged by later carpenters as a great master craftsman for his devotion to technological innovation.

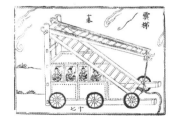

"Cloud ladder" used in sieges, inventor said to be Lu Ban

The philosopher Heraclitus (*c*. 540-480 BC) of ancient Greece developed dialectic thought.

c. 509 BC: The end of the monarchy in ancient Rome and the start of the Roman Republic.

494 BC

486 BC

King Goujian of Yue conquered the State of Wu by perseverance

Construction of Han Gou

Spring and Autumn Annals

▶ In 494 BC, the State of Yue in the Yangtze River region was defeated by its powerful neighboring country, the State of Wu. King Goujian of Yue pretended to be compliant, but he resolved to take revenge. To remind himself of the humiliation, King Goujian hung some gall to taste before every meal and slept on sticks and straw, determined to restore his kingdom. Finally in 482 BC, the State of Yue wiped out the State of Wu, and became the new power.

Sword of King
Goujian of Yue

▶ In 486 BC, during the late Spring and Autumn Period, King Fuchai of Wu, ventured north in his contention for supremacy. He ordered the construction of Han City (now Yangzhou) and Han Gou (Han Conduit), a canal connecting the Yangtze River northwards to the Huaihe River by means of existing waterways, lakes, and marshes. Han Gou was the earliest section of the later Grand Canal.

▶ As the earliest chronicle in China, the *Spring and Autumn Annals* chronologically recorded the history of various states from 722 to 481 BC. The contents covered the vassal states' diplomatic relations, alliances and military actions, births, deaths, and marriages among ruling families, as well as rituals, city construction, hunting expeditions, and farm land management. The chronicle also noted natural disasters and phenomena such as floods, earthquakes, pestilence, constellations and eclipses. Originally a historical text arranged on annalistic principles of the State of Lu, the *Spring and Autumn Annals* was eventually edited and complied by Confucius, and became revered as a Confucian classic. Due to its conciseness, a number of commentaries were composed to explain its meaning.

◎ 490 BC: The Persian Wars (the Battle of Marathon) broke out. Athenian herald Pheidippides was sent to Sparta to request help, after the Persians landed at Marathon, Greece. He ran a distance of 240 km in 48 hours, thus originating the "Marathon" race.

The Warring States Period (476-221 BC)

The second half of the Eastern Zhou is known historically as the Warring States Period. In this period, wars were frequently fought between vassal states. To defeat others, every state became actively engaged in economic development, and the iron-casting industry flourished through farming tools production, along with irrigation projects, commerce and trade, and handicraft industry. Philosophical development was evident in the "Hundred Schools of Thought." The many capital cities were no longer mere local political centers, but gradually became also financial centers. These development trends and the strengthening of financial and cultural ties between different states laid a solid foundation for the birth of a unified country.

Yingyuan, gold pieces used in the State of Chu

Bubi, spade-shaped coins circulated in the states of Jin, Eastern Zhou, and Western Zhou

Wooden warrior holding a sword of the Warring States Period

Daobi, knife-shaped coins circulated in the states of Qi, Zhao and Yan

The adoption of metal currency

During the Warring States Period, metal currency became popular due to development in trade and coinage techniques. Currency in this period is generally classified into five categories: daobi (knife-shaped coin), bubi (spade-shaped coin), huanqian (circular coin with center hollow square), yibiqian (shell-shaped coin), and yingyuan (gold piece). These forms of currency circulated in different regions, resulting in inconveniences in trade between the states.

○ The Greek historian Herodotus (c. 484-425 BC) composed The Histories, the first work of history in Western literature.

○ The Greek historian Thucydides (c. 471-400 BC) wrote History of the Peloponnesian War.

○ The Greek philosopher Socrates (469-339 BC) proposed self-cognizance, the "midwife" analogy, and the ethical argument that "virtue is knowledge."

Mozi

Facsimile of Mozi

Mo Di (480-390 BC), styled Mozi, was a great thinker of the Warring States Period. He denounced offensive warfare between vassal states, and aspired to establish a society of equality. He also criticized extravagant living and hereditary official posts among the nobility. He proposed the concepts of universal love among people, pacifism in diplomacy, frugality in life, and meritocracy in government. Regarded as the founder of Mohism, Mozi cultivated many disciples, and composed *Mozi*, a book on his beliefs and philosophy.

Analects of Confucius

Many years after his death, the disciples of Confucius compiled his words and acts into the *Analects of Confucius*, a record of the great thinker's philosophical discussions on matters of humanism, ethics, education, state affairs management and other themes, in 20 chapters. Regarded as a classic by later scholars, the book was said to have so much power that "one could rule with half of it."

Confucius Preaching

The Han, Zhao and Wei families divided the State of Jin

Jin was one of the many vassal states under the Zhou Dynasty in the Spring and Autumn Period. During the reign of Duke Xian, other clans outside the Jin royal family became engaged in state administration. These clans developed into the ten ministerial families in the mid Spring and Autumn Period, holding the real reins of powers within Jin. By the late Spring and Autumn Period, only six clans survived, collectively known as the "Six Ministerial Families," namely the Han, Wei, Zhao, Fan, Zhi and Zhonghang families. In 453 BC, the Han, Zhao and Wei families eliminated the Zhi family and divided its territory, becoming the three power-holders of the State of Jin. In 403 BC, the King of Zhou had to recognize the three family fiefdoms as separate vassal states, marking the ultimate division of the State of Jin. The nominal State of Jin was ended by the three powers in 376 BC.

◎ The Greek philosopher Democritus (*c*. 460- 370 BC) proposed the Atomist theory and the hypothesis of images or idols (*eidola*) in epistemology.

◎ 451 BC: Enacted in the Roman Republic, the *Law of the Twelve Tables* was considered the first written law codes in ancient Rome, introducing Roman laws.

Li Kui and his reforms

Li Kui (?-395 BC) was a legalist politician in the early Warring States Period. In 445 BC, as prime minister, Li carried out a series of reforms in the State of Wei. To improve the economy, he encouraged agricultural production and adopted food price-control measures. In government administration, he advocated the abolition of hereditary titles and awarding official posts and money to those who contributed to the state. Centralization of power in the ruler was also stressed. Acknowledged as the founder of Legalism, Li was also credited with the compilation of *Book of Law*, the first systemized codification of laws in Chinese history, serving as an example for the constitutions of Qin and other states. Under Li Kui's reforms, the State of Wei quickly rose economically and militarily as one of the powers of the early Warring State Period.

Bian Que

Bian Que, a native of the State of Qi, was a renowned physician in the time between the Spring and Autumn Period and the Warring States Period. From the practices of his predecessors, Bian Que originated the four-step diagnosis of "Looking (at tongues and exteriors), Listening (to voice and breathing patterns), Inquiring (about symptoms), and Taking (pulse)." He also used needles, stones and other prototype medical devices in treatment. His four-step diagnosis and medical devices still in use today, Bian Que is revered as the "father of Traditional Chinese Medicine."

Eastern Han stone relief of Bian Que treating patients with acupuncture needles; the bird-like figure at the top right corner is Bian Que.

○ 443-429 BC: During the leadership of the Athenian statesman Pericles (*c.* 495-429 BC), the city enjoyed its golden age of Athenian democracy.

○ 431-404 BC: The Peloponnesian War.

○ The Greek philosopher Plato (427-347 BC) founded the Academy, and established his philosophical system centered on "Platonic Idealism."

Seven Warring States

Zuo Zhuan
(Commentary of Zuo)

Battle scenes carved on bronze vessels
of the Warring States Period

Portrait of Zuo Qiuming

By the early Warring States Period, most small vassal states had been annexed. The remaining major powers were: Qin in the west, Jin in the north, Qi and Yan in the east, and Chu and Wu in the south. Among the supreme states, Jin, Qi, Chu and Yue were the most powerful. The states of Han, Zhao and Wei rose to power after dividing the State of Jin. In 386 BC, the State of Qi, which changed its ruling family from the Jiang to the Tian clan, was recognized as a vassal state by the Zhou court, and joined the states of Qin, Chu, Zhao, Wei, Han and Yan to form the Seven Warring States. During the following years, these states fought numerous battles and campaigns for domination, annexing and being annexed. In the end, the State of Qin eliminated all the other six states and unified China for the first time in Chinese history.

Composed by Zuo Qiuming in the late Spring and Autumn Period, *Zuo Zhuan* is a commentary on the *Spring and Autumn Annals*. The book recorded the decline of the royal family of Zhou, the history of the vassal states competing for supremacy, as well as a range of information on rituals and etiquettes, social conventions and customs, regulations and systems, ethical and moral standards, astronomy and geography, calendars, ancient documents, myths and tales, ballads and proverbs. Among the many aspects depicted, the description of warfare and important figures is the most significant.

Mencius

Mengzi (385-304 BC), a native of Zouyi (now Shandong), developed Confucius' concept of "benevolence" into the idea of "benevolent government." Acknowledged as the most influential philosopher after Confucius, his thoughts were elaborated in *Mengzi*. Mengzi argued the necessity of "private property" for a benevolent government, and proposed that "the people are the most important element, the state next, and the sovereign the least." He also believed that every individual is born with the good qualities of *ren* (benevolence), *yi* (righteousness), *li* (etiquette) and *zhi* (aptitude), but it depended on cultivation and environment to develop such qualities.

Portrait of Mencius

Zhuangzi and his book

Portrait of Zhuangzi

Zhuangzi (360-290 BC), a native of the State of Song, was a representative figure of Daoism in the Warring States Period. He lived in seclusion, and argued for restoring of the self to the original states of life, rather than pursuing wealth and glory or diligently serving the country. The book *Zhuangzi* was poetical in language and imaginative in content. In a chapter named "Enjoying Untroubled Ease," he made analogies between the roc and the turtle-dove, as well as between the *da chun* (long-living tree) and the mushroom, to illustrate his idea that nothing is able to surpass its own nature or the environment. He also made the proposition that humans should equally enjoy traveling freely in spiritual worlds and boundlessly beyond reality.

○ The Greek philosopher Aristotle (*c.* 384-322 BC) inspired the Peripatetic School, proposed the concept of substance (*ousia*) in his *Metaphysics*, and originated research on logic, ethics, politics and biology.

Shang Yang's reforms

Star Manual of Masters Gan and Shi

In 359 and 350 BC, Shang Yang (*c.* 390-338 BC) enacted reforms in the State of Qin. He established a punishment system in which people grouped (5 to 10 families) with the perpetrator were also punished. He also broke large clans into nuclear families, by creating a double tax on households with more than one son. He started the noble rank system, divided the country into prefectures, standardized measurements, and abolished the well-field system so land could be sold. Shang's reforms changed Qin into a powerful state, but infringed on the interests of the old nobility. In the end, Shang Yang was executed and the reforms halted. For its indispensable contributions to the rise of the State of Qin and the tragic end of its mastermind, the Shang Yang Reform is remembered as the most important among the many reforms during the Spring and Autumn and the Warring States periods.

As the world's first astronomical writings, *Star Manual of Masters Gan and Shi* is the collective name for *Astronomical Star Observations* by Gan De from the State of Chu and *Astronomy* by Shi Shen from the State of Wei. The book was allegedly compiled in mid-4th century BC. The two astronomers made relatively accurate observations of the five major planets: Venus, Jupiter, Mercury, Mars and Saturn. They also recorded the names of 800 stars, positioned 121 stars, and recognized the phenomenon of eclipse. Compiled from their observations, *Star Catalogue of Gan and Shi* is the earliest star catalogue in the world.

© The Greek philosopher Epicurus (*c.* 341-270 BC) founded Epicureanism, and expounded the theory of "motions and interactions of atoms moving through empty space," and originated the idea of "Social Contract."

Qu Yuan and his poem *Li Sao*

King Wuling of Zhao adopted "Hu uniforms and mounted archery"

Portrait of
Qu Yuan

Qu Yuan (*c*. 339-278 BC) was a minister in the State of Chu with an important position. However, the Chu king fell under the influence of other corrupt, jealous ministers who slandered Qu Yuan, and banished the most loyal counselor to a place called Xiang. In 278 BC, the State of Chu was conquered by the powerful Qin. Hearing the news, Qu Yuan waded into the Miluo River while holding a huge rock to commit ritual suicide for his country. As a great poet, he wrote *Li Sao* (*The Lament*), the longest poem in ancient China.

Sculpture of man in
Hu uniform practicing
mounted archery

"Hu" was the collective name given to northwestern nomadic tribes of ancient China. In 307 BC, King Wuling of Zhao (r. 325-299 BC) ordered the abandoning of traditional robes and the adoption of Hu uniforms. The purpose of the reform was to enhance the army's mobility by replacing the original infantry and chariots with cavalry archers. The widely praised reforms of King Wuling turned the State of Zhao into a powerful country with large areas of territory gained from the north.

Li Sao

In the first part of the poem, Qu Yuan expressed his fervent concern over the fate of the State of Chu, as well as hopes for political reforms. In the second part, the patriotic author described the quest, sorrow and disillusionment of an exiled minister of state. The poem carries typical features of romanticism in its structural magnificence, literary grace, mythic allusions, and imaginative analogy like the beauty and vanilla. The poem was so great that people identified the "Style of *Li Sao*," which had profound influence on later poetry.

Facsimile of
Li Sao

Models of
bronze boots

○ 336 BC: Alexander the Great succeeded to the throne of Macedon. From 334 to 324 BC, he led his army eastwards to conquer Persia, Central Asia and India, known as one of the most famous expeditions in ancient history. In 331 BC, he established Alexander's Empire. He died in 323 BC.

○ The Greek mathematician Euclid (*c*. 330-275 BC) wrote *Elements*, the greatest geometrical work in ancient Greece.

"Vertical and horizontal alliance" strategy

Zou Yan and the theory of "Five Elements"

Xunzi

Portrait of Xunzi

Xunzi (340-245 BC), a native of the State of Zhao, was a renowned Confucian philosopher of the Warring States Period. He believed that humans are innately bad or corrupt, and that "so-called good men are only pretending to be good." He asserted that the evil nature of man should be changed through education and environment. He also argued that *li* (ritual or protocol) is the highest standard of measurement and the foundation of state affairs management. He further argued that a combination of rituals and laws should be adopted to maintain social hierarchy and the feudal system. His book, *The Xunzi* commented and summarized various schools of thoughts in the Warring States Period.

In the turbulent Warring States Period, intellectuals devoted themselves to studying diplomacy and military strategy, trying to persuade the rulers of various states to adopt their strategies. Among the intellectuals, Su Qin (?-234 BC) and Zhang Yi (?-310 BC) were two outstanding figures. Su Qin advocated alliances with small countries to guard against annexation by a powerful nation, while Zhang Yi advocated attacking small countries through alliance with a powerful nation to expand territory. Their strategies were collectively known in Chinese historical writings as the "vertical and horizontal alliance" strategies.

A new theory combining the Yin-Yang and Five Elements theories was promoted by Zou Yan (*c*. 305-240 BC), a representative figure of the Yin-Yang School (of Naturalists) in the late Warring States Period. Based on spatial correspondence, the theory offered new explanations for universal mechanisms and changes in society and sovereignty. Zou Yan believed the material world is composed of the Five Elements (metal, wood, water, fire and earth), which generate or destroy each other in cycles. He further argued that social changes were influenced by the cycles of the Five Elements.

◎ *c*. 323-187 BC: The Maurya Empire in ancient India.

◎ 312-64 BC: The Seleucid Empire period in Central and West Asia.

◎ The Greek astronomer and mathematician Aristarchus (*c*. 310-230 BC) first proposed the "Heliocentric Model," in which the Earth revolves around the Sun as well as rotating around its own axis.

◎ 305-30 BC: The Ptolemaic Dynasty in ancient Egypt.

● Accommodating *Shi*

● *Han Feizi*

● The Battle of Changping

Facsimile of
Han Feizi

● *Shi* was the collective name for intellectuals in ancient China. In the Warring States Period, it was a popular practice to keep intellectuals at one's home. Rulers and prominent clans accommodated people with special talent as their retainers, whom they consulted on various matters. In this way, they spread their political reputation and influence.

● In mid-3rd century BC, a series of theories on state affairs management were proposed, with *Han Feizi* as the representative work. Composed by Han Feizi (280-233 BC), the 55-chapter book elucidated the philosophy of Legalism. Han Feizi advocated a stable social structure based on classes, in which the emperor was supreme in status and absolute in power, and where the officials performed their duties under regulations, while the subjects lived under the laws. In his legal system, every one would be equal before the law.

● In 262 BC, the State of Zhao sent troops to aid the State of Han, under attack from the powerful Qin. The two sides fought at Changping (now northwest Gaoping, Shanxi), and the battle resulted in a stalemate, lasting for three years. In 260 BC, the Qin feigned a retreat, and cut off Zhao's supplies. With no reinforcements coming, over 400,000 Zhao soldiers surrendered after 46 days of starvation. The Qin general buried alive all the Zhao soldiers, and the State of Zhao's power was severely weakened.

○ 4th century BC - 4th century AD: The ancient Indian epics *Mahabharata* and *Ramayana* were composed.

○ The Greek mathematician and physicist Archimedes (*c.* 287-212 BC) composed *The Measurement of a Circle*, the greatest mathematical work in ancient Greece.

○ *c.* 269-232 BC: During the reign of Asoka the Great, the Maurya Empire entered its zenith period.

256 BC

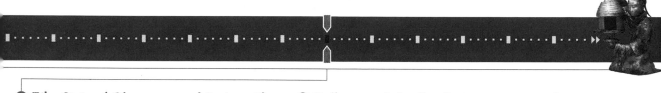

● Tthe State of Qin conquered Eastern Zhou   ● Dujiangyan Irrigation System constructed by Li Bing and his son

● In 256 BC, Qin general Ying Jiu captured Yangcheng (now Dengfeng, Henan) in the State of Han, and then swept over 20 prefectures in the State of Zhao, killing over 100,000 people. Ji Yan, King Nan of Zhou, was terrified. He plotted with the kings of Yan and Zhao in seeking a military alliance with other states against Qin. However, the plot was leaked. The powerful Qin army attacked the Zhou capital Luoyang and took King Nan captive. He was later released, but died soon after. The death of King Nan marked the end of the 879-year-long Zhou Dynasty, whose territory and cities were annexed into the State of Qin.

The still-operating Dujiangyan Irrigation System

● In 256 BC, during the reign of King Zhaoxiang of Qin, Li Bing (302-235 BC), the magistrate of Chengdu, together with his son directed the construction of the Dujiangyan Irrigation System. After much investigation, Li Bing decided to divide the Min River into two streams, allowing one stream to continue on its normal course, while the other stream would flow into farm fields in the Chengdu Plain. The Dujiangyan project made use of flood waters to irrigate farmlands, and turned the Chengdu Plain into "the most productive agricultural area" in ancient China. The Dujiangyan Irrigation System is still functioning as the oldest surviving irrigation project without a dam.

◎ 264-241 BC: The First Punic War
◎ 247 BC - AD 226: The Parthian Empire in ancient Iran.

▶ **Lü Buwei and *Lüshi Chunqiu***

▶ **Jing Ke the assassin**

Facsimile of *Lüshi Chunqiu (Master Lü's Spring and Autumn Annals)*

▶ Lü Buwei (*c*. 292-235 BC) was from Puyang in the State of Wei (now southern Puyang, Henan) in the late Warring States Period. Originally a successful merchant, Lü later served as Prime Minister for King Zhuangxiang of Qin. When King Zheng (later Qin Shi Huang) ascended the throne at a young age, Lü remained in his post, wielding real power as a regent. During his regency, a solid foundation was laid for the unification of China by the State of Qin. Compiled in 239 BC by follows of Lü, *Master Lü's Spring and Autumn Annals* was a masterpiece of the Miscellaneous School. It was composed of 160 articles in 26 volumes, totaling over 200,000 Chinese characters. Upholding Daoist principles, the book absorbed merits from the schools of Confucianism, Legalism, Mohism and the Military, to form comprehensive systems for politics, economics, philosophy, ethics, and the military. The book served as a summary of past experiences for Qin rulers to consult.

▶ In 227 BC, the State of Yan made a final effort to assassinate Ying Zheng, the King of Qin. Jing Ke (?-227 BC), the assassin, arrived in Qin with a dagger hidden inside a rolled-up map of Yan. At the palace, Jing Ke unrolled the map, seized the dagger and plunged it towards the King of Qin. He missed, and was killed on the spot. Enraged, the King of Qin immediately sent his general Wang Jian to wipe out the State of Yan. The allied troops of Yan and Zhao fought the Qin troops at Yishui, but were defeated. The State of Yan was thus eliminated.

Stone relief of Jing Ke's attempt to assassinate the King of Qin

Silk Painting

Painting of a lady with
a dragon and a phoenix

● Silk was the material for writing and painting, before paper was invented in China. Artists of that time portrayed on silk images of beasts and birds, people and deities, and mythical animals. Silk painting emerged in the Warring States Period, and fully developed during the Western Han Dynasty.

In February 1949, a 31.2cm x 23.2cm silk painting was unearthed from a tomb of the State of Chu (now Changsha, Hubei). In the painting, a traditionally robed woman is a Zen pose; over her head is a flying phoenix with curling tail feathers; and beside the phoenix, a curved dragon soars into the sky. Then 24 years later, another silk painting, 37.5cm x 28cm, was unearthed. The painting portrayed a man wearing a "*guan*" (coronet-shaped traditional Chinese hat) and holding a sword in one hand and reins in the other, riding on a boat-shaped dragon. The first painting is now known as "A Lady with a Dragon and a Phoenix," and the latter "A Man Riding on a Dragon." The excavation of the two silk paintings is not only proof of the use of silk as a material for writing and paintings in the Warring States Period, but also marked the achievements in painting of the time.

Painting of man
riding a dragon

Huangdi Neijing (Internal Canon of the Yellow Emperor)

Facsimile of *Huangdi Neijing* (*Internal Canon of the Yellow Emperor*)

● Regarded as the earliest medical text in ancient China as well as one of the four "Classics of Chinese Medicine," *Huangdi Neijing* was attributed to its legendary author, the Yellow Emperor. In actuality, it is a chronological summary of medical treatments and theories by various physicians from the Spring and Autumn Period, rather than singly authored. Based on ancient Chinese philosophical theories, the book discusses their applications in medical practice, such as the theories of Yin-Yang and Five Elements, of pulse (*mai*), of channels and collaterals (*jingluo*), and basic theories on diagnostics, treatment, and maintaining health.

221 - 206 BC

Qin Dynasty
Qin Shi Huang, the First Emperor (r. 221-210 BC)

The unification of China in 221 BC, under the First Emperor Qin Shi Huang, marked the beginning of Imperial China. To consolidate his rule, Qin Shi Huang enacted various reforms. First, centralization of power was established, with judicial, executive and military powers lying in the hands of the emperor. Second, the county system was enforced to govern administrative regions throughout the country. Third, the forms of written characters were unified and standardized. Fourth, currency was standardized to "*banliangqian*" (coins weighing 2.8-8.1 g); and measurements of length, weight and volume were unified. Other measures included construction of expressways, application of new laws, and many others. However, the Qin Dynasty lasted only 15 years before it was replaced by the Han Dynasty. The reasons for its decline might be traced in its repressive measures, ruthless law codes, and continual military expeditions.

Portrait of Ying Zheng, the First Emperor of Qin

Known as the First Emperor of China, Qin Shi Huang (or Ying Zheng) was born in 259 BC, and ascended the throne in 246 BC at the age of 13. He was king under a regent until 238 BC, when at the age of 21 he assumed full power. In the nine years that followed, Qin Shi Huang conquered the states of Han, Zhao, Wei, Chu, Yan and Qi. The first unified state of China was established in 221 BC. Under the name the "First Emperor," Qin Shi Huang centralized power, and enacted various reforms to develop the economy and consolidate his reign. In 210 BC, he died on a journey to the east of the country. Huhai, his second son, ascended the throne.

The Terracotta Army

Discovered in 1974 in Lintong (Xi'an, Shaanxi), near the Mausoleum of the First Emperor Qin Shi Huang, the Terracotta Army contains more than 8,000 terracotta warriors and horses, in addition to a large number of war chariots and weapons, excavated in three of the many tomb pits by the main tomb. The terracotta warriors were distinctive in facial expressions, hairstyles, and dressed according to ranks and duties. With generals, infantries, cavalries, archers, and other divisions, the stunning underground army is considered a replica of the imperial guards of the First Emperor.

Terracotta archer in half-kneeling position

Bronze horse-pulled war chariot

Clay tiles and eave tiles of the Qin

Using clay as construction material dated back to the Shang Dynasty, mainly seen in the production of clay drainage pipes; and in the early Western Zhou, clay was used to make plain tiles, pan tiles, and eave tiles. During the Qin, the most significant feature in construction was using clay floor tiles and eaves tiles with different decorative patterns. Floor tiles were produced according to the building design, with decorative patterns on the surface, while most eaves tiles were round in shape and emblazoned, ranging in diameter from 10-40 cm.

220 BC

The construction of highways by Qin Shi Huang

Lingqu Canal

In 220 BC, Qin Shi Huang ordered the construction of national roads extending to the north, northeast, east and southeast of the capital city Xianyang. Historically referred to as "run way," these 50m-wide roads were built above ground level with multiple layers of rammed earth. Of the three lanes of a road, the central lane was reserved for imperial vehicles, while the two side lanes were for public use. The dual purposes of laying highways were: first, to increase the mobility of troops in case remnant forces of the six states revolted; second, to link the whole country with strengthened economic and cultural ties.

After unifying the six states in the north, Qin Shi Huang began his campaign to conquer the southern Baiyue peoples in the provinces of Zhejiang, Fujian, Guangdong, and Guangxi. However, little headway was made after three years of endeavor, due to the complex terrain delaying supplies. In 214 BC, Qin Shi Huang ordered the construction of the Lingqu Canal, connecting the Xiangjiang and Lishui rivers, and the larger Yangtze and Pearl river waters. After construction was finished, the Qin armies were supported by a steady flow of abundant supplies, and the southern regions were annexed as Qin territory. Built for military purposes, the Lingqu Canal remains as one of the oldest irrigation systems in the world.

The remains of a Qin Dynasty highway in Shaanxi Province

218- 201 BC: Carthage lost the Second Punic War, and became a tributary state of Rome.

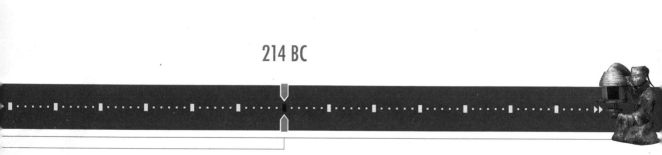

The Great Wall of China in the Qin Dynasty

Scene of war at the Great Wall

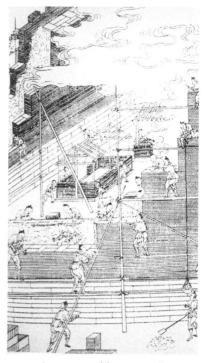

Construction of the Great Wall

In 214 BC, the First Emperor Qin Shi Huang ordered the construction of an immense defensive wall, for whose construction nearly a million men were mobilized. Linking several walls already existing in Qin, Zhao and Yan since the time of the Warring States, the Great Wall stretched over approximately 5,000 km, from Jieshi, Liaodong, in the east to Lintao (now Minxian County, Gansu) in the west, bordering the Yin Mountains in the north. To guard against aggression from nomadic tribes in northern and western China, fortresses were constructed at strategic positions, with garrison troops, along the Great Wall. Intended as a barrier separating the sedentary Han population from the nomadic steppe people, the great wall turned out be a witness to national amalgamation, and cultural and economic exchange between the two communities.

◎ 215-205 BC: The First Macedonian War.

213 BC   209 BC

● Burning of books and burial of scholars (213-212 BC)

● In 213 BC, dissatisfied with the tyranny of the emperor and the abolishment of the enfeoffment system, some scholars cited Confucian classics to satirize current policies and slander the government. To stabilize the newly unified country, Qin Shi Huang ordered the Confucian classics be burned along with works of the "Hundred Schools of Thought"; the only books spared were the *History of Qin*, and those on medicine, agriculture and divination. This event was known in history as "the book burning." The following year, enraged by alchemists who had failed to find the "elixir of life" and scholars who continued to vilify his policies, Qin Shi Huang buried 460 alchemists and Confucian scholars alive at Xianyang, referred to as "the burial of scholars."

● Dazexiang Uprising

● In 209 BC, Chen Sheng and Wu Guang, both military captains, were ordered to lead 900 newly enlisted soldiers to Yuyang (now north Beijing) as a garrison to defend the northern border. Due to heavy rainfall, they were held up in Dazexiang, Jixian County, and it became obvious that they could not arrive on time. According to the law, they would be executed no matter what the reason. Knowing that they were doomed, Chen Sheng and Wu Guang led their soldiers to start a rebellion. They killed the army official, and captured all of Jixian County, marking the beginning of peasant uprisings in the late Qin Dynasty. This event came to be known as the first peasant uprising in Chinese history.

● Xiang Yu

Portrait of Xiang Yu

● Xiang Ji (233-202 BC), styled Yu, was born to a military family. He rallied an army in 209 BC, and the next year followed the example of Chen Sheng and Wu Guang's revolt against the Qin. Xiang Yu won a series of victories in battle, and in 207 BC destroyed the main force of the Qin army at Julu. However, defeated by Liu Bang (later emperor of the Han Dynasty) in a crucial battle in 202 BC, Xiang Yu committed suicide by the Wu River.

Battle of Julu

Liu Bang

Chu-Han Contention (206-202 BC)

In 207 BC, Xiang Yu led 50,000 men to Julu (now southwest Pingxiang, Hebei Province) to relieve the besieged anti-Qin forces in the former territory of Zhao. Xiang sent one subordinate commander with 20,000 men across the Zhanghe River to cut off the Qin army's food supply. After they crossed the river, the small regiment sank their boats, carrying food only for three days, showing their determination to fight to the death. Imbued with high morale, the Chu soldiers won nine successive battles and claimed a glorious victory over the Qin army.

Portrait of Liu Bang

Liu Bang (256-195 BC) was a native of Pei (now Peixian County, Jiangsu) in the Warring States Period. In 209 BC, following Chen Sheng's revolt against the Qin, Liu Bang joined the cause and became a main force. After capturing Qin's capital Xianyang and its periphery two years later, Liu Bang abolished the Qin cruel laws, ruled his troops with discipline, and was loved by the people. In the same year, Xiang Yu took control over Guanzhong, and titled Liu Bang "King of Han." In the five years that followed, Liu Bang grew more powerful, and was able to contend against Xiang Yu for supremacy. After defeating Xiang Yu, Liu Bang proclaimed himself Emperor of China in 202 BC, and established the Han Dynasty.

While Xiang Yu was engaged in the Battle of Julu fighting the major forces of the Qin, Liu Bang took the opportunity to capture Xianyang, baring his ambitions in the Guanzhong region (now central Shaanxi). Liu's counterpart, Xiang Yu, the self-proclaimed "Overlord of Western Chu," established his regime in Pengcheng (now Xuzhou, Jiangsu Province). Liu was enfeoffed with impoverished territory in Hanzhong (southwest Shaanxi) and Sichuan. In 206 BC, Liu reentered Guanzhong to reclaim his rightful territory, and the Chu-Han Contention was forged. In 202 BC, Liu Bang won a final victory over Xiang Yu, and established the Han Dynasty.

● Battle of Gaixia ● Western Han Dynasty

Silk painting from
a Han tomb

● Originally a subordinate of Xiang Yu, Liu Bang gradually assumed enough power to contend against Xiang Yu. In 203 BC, the two sides agreed that the two states of Chu and Han would coexist peacefully along the border of Honggou (now east Henan). While Xiang Yu was moving his troops back east of Honggou, Liu Bang launched an attack and besieged Chu troops at Gaixia (now southeast Lingbi, Anhui). Liu Bang ordered his soldiers to sing Chu songs, evoking in the Chu troops longing for their families back home, greatly reducing their will to fight. Although Xiang Yu broke through the entrapment and escaped to the Wu River where he could return to Chu territory, he committed suicide, being too ashamed to face his own people. Liu Bang thus won the final victory in battle.

Changxin Palace Lantern

● The Han Dynasty is divided into two periods: the Western Han from 206 BC to 25 AD, centered in Chang'an; and the Eastern Han from 25 AD to 220 AD, centered in Luoyang. With vast territory, the Western Han was the most prosperous multi-national state in Asia at that time. Philosophically, the emperors of the Han Dynasty advocated the "Mandate of Heaven" to consolidate their rule. Centralized administration was institutionalized mid-dynasty during the rule of Emperor Wu. The "Silk Road," a caravan and mercantile transport route stretching to West Asia, was established. This period is recognized as the Han "golden age," during which the economy and culture flourished, and the empire's political influence reached far into West Asia. At the end of the Western Han, Wang Mang, nephew of Grand Empress Dowager Wang, was proclaimed acting emperor. During his 15-year rule, the Western Han gradually declined, with social turmoil and extensive peasant revolts.

Battle of Baideng

Empress Lü Zhi seized the court (195-180 BC)

Han Dynasty capital of Chang'an (194-104 BC)

In 201 BC, Modu Chanyu of Xiongnu (emperor of the nomadic Xiongnu Empire) invaded the northern Han territory of China, and further besieged Jinyang (now Taiyuan, Shanxi). Liu Bang, or Han Emperor Gao, led an army of 300,000 soldiers to fight off the Xiongnu troops, but was trapped at Baideng Mountain (now northeast Datong, Shanxi) for a drawn-out seven days. Unable to stop the Xiongnu aggression at its northern borders, the Han Dynasty reluctantly resorted to a humiliating *heqin* (marriage alliance) strategy, marrying off its princesses to the Xiongnu emperors. This *heqin* practice lasted for more than 50 years, before Emperor Wu finally forced the Xiongnu out of Han territory and restored peace on the northwestern borders by peace treaties with the Xiongnu emperor.

Lü Zhi (241-180 BC) was the wife of Liu Bang, or the Han Emperor Gao. Shortly after the establishment of the Han Dynasty, she assisted her husband to eliminate several vassals who had been awarded principalities for their contributions to the state's founding. After Liu Bang's death in 195 BC, Emperor Hui was enthroned, but real power rested in the hands of the now Empress Dowager Lü. Upon Emperor Hui's death in 187 BC, Lü Zhi took over the court as regent, gave titles to many of her nephews as vassals, and controlled the army to guarantee her authority. Despite her usurpation, Empress Lü Zhi, continuing the "recuperation policy" enacted by Liu Bang, restored and developed the national economy.

Construction of the Han capital Chang'an (now northwest Xi'an city) began in 194 BC, and the city wall was completed in 190 BC. In 104 BC, Emperor Wu of Han ordered the construction of a series of palaces: the Northern Palace, Gui Palace, Mingguang Palace, Jianzhang Palace, and Shanglin Gardens in the city's west. Upon the completion of these buildings, the Han capital of Chang'an took the shape of an irregular square with a perimeter of 25.7 km, covering an area of 36 sq km. The 8 main streets and 160 lanes crisscrossing inside the city divided Chang'an into 9 districts. At its height, the city supported a population of 300,000 people, and is recognized as the first metropolis in Chinese history.

The Han Tombs at Mawangdui

Rule of Wen and Jing (179-141 BC)

In the 1970s, three family tombs of the Marquis of Dai, Li Cang from the early Western Han Dynasty, were excavated at Mawangdui, Changsha, Hunan Province. A total of 3,000 artifacts were unearthed, including silk garments, lacquerware, pottery vessels, bamboo writings, seals, agricultural and animal products, Chinese herbal medicine, three maps and two silk paintings. Classic texts of *I Ching* (*Book of Changes*), *Laozi* (*Daodejing*), *Prescriptions for 52 Diseases* and other texts were found at the site, totaling 120,000 characters in over 20 books. Besides the above artifacts, a well-preserved corpse was also found, which is believed to be that of Lady Dai, wife of the Marquis.

Robe made of plain silk gauze

The silk garments excavated reveal fine craftsmanship in their delicate coloring, intricate patterns and exquisite workmanship. Among the textiles is a 48-gm robe made of plain silk gauze, with a 195-cm horizontal span across the two sleeves and 128-cm long from collar to bottom. As thin as the wings of cicadas, the gown can be folded to fit into the hand.

Portrait of Emperor Wen of Han

The Rule of Wen and Jing refers to the successive 40-year reigns of the two emperors, which brought stability and prosperity to the country. Learning a lesson from the collapse of the Qin Dynasty, the two emperors abolished harsh laws, pardoned criminals and reduced taxation, to help recover and develop the economy. Under these policies, the population increased and society developed. The two emperors also weakened or eliminated lords with principalities and various privileges, and finally pacified the "Rebellion of the Seven Princes" in 154 BC. The Rule of Wen and Jing has been widely praised in Chinese history.

Portrait of Emperor Jing of Han

© 200-197 BC: The Second Macedonian War.

154 BC

● *Faults of the Qin*, by Jia Yi   ● **Rebellion of the Seven Princes**

● Jia Yi (200-168 BC), a native of Luoyang, was already celebrated for his poetry and essay writing ability by the age of 18. In his early 20s, Jia Yi was appointed by Emperor Wen of Han as "Learned Scholar," to preach Confucian classics, and then promoted to an even higher position. However, later slandered and demoted, he committed suicide at the age of 33. Jia Yi was famous for his many poems and writings, the most notable essay being *Faults of the Qin*. It contains two chapters of brilliant parallelism and hyperbole to explain the faults of the Qin, as well as to remind Han emperors of the importance of learning from history.

Portrait of Jia Yi

● At the beginning of the Han Dynasty, while continuing the Qin jurisdiction system, Liu Bang granted principalities to more than 10 relatives and meritorious generals (of his own clan and different clans), bringing chaos to the country. To consolidate his rule, Liu Bang eliminated lords with different surnames, keeping only those of his own clan. The power of the Liu princes grew so rapidly, that it threatened the central government. In 154 BC, Liu Bi, prince of Wu, and Liu Dai, prince of Chu, formed an alliance with other five princes, and revolted against the government in the name of "eradicating evils around the emperor." Emperor Jing led the army to suppress the revolt, but Liu Bi would not surrender and even proclaimed himself the "Eastern Emperor." Within three months, Liu Bi was defeated and killed by Emperor Jing.

Terracotta warriors from the tomb of Liu Dai, King of Chu

◎ 171-168 BC: Rome conquered Macedon after the Third Macedonian War.
◎ 149-148 BC: Macedon launched the Fourth Macedonian War to overthrow Roman rule, but failed.
◎ 149-146 BC: Rome conquered Carthage after the Third Punic War, and made it a province.

● Chao Cuo

● Han Emperor Wu (r. 141-87 BC)

Portrait of Emperor
Wu of Han

● Chao Cuo (200-154 BC), advisor and vice prime minister of Han Emperor Jing, was a practical statesman with the nickname of "brainpower." On relations with the Xiongnu, after summarizing past strategies and tactics, Chao Cuo proposed transferring people to inhabit the border areas and adopting an active defense policy. On agricultural production, he advocated the policies of "agriculture first" and "grain exchange for official posts." On military affairs, he suggested that Emperor Jing reduce the size of principalities to weaken the power of the lords, so as to consolidate his reign. Emperor Jing took his advice, but the actions caused a joint rebellion of the seven principalities. Chao Cuo was then killed for his recommendations.

● Liu Che (157-87 BC), the fifth emperor of the Han Dynasty, ascended the throne at the young age of 16 in 141 BC; his reign signified the turning point of the Western Han. Domestically, Emperor Wu continued to reduce the remnant influence of the enfeoffment system. Philosophically, he highlighted the superior status of Confucianism, and reinforced the sovereignty concept of the "Mandate of Heaven." Economically, he made national monopolies of currency minting, salt and iron production and trade, and appointed officials to control commodity prices. He also exerted great efforts to harness the Yellow River, and constructed irrigation systems. Beginning in 133 BC, Emperor Wu launched a series of campaigns against the Xiongnu Empire, ultimately eradicating their threat. In 138 and 119 BC, he dispatched Zhang Qian twice as an imperial envoy to the Western Regions, ensuring the safety of the "Silk Road." This series of measures taken by Emperor Wu consolidated his rule, and further expanded Han territory.

Fu, a new literary genre, and fu master Sima Xiangru

Facsimiles of *Zixu Fu*
and *Shanglin Fu*

The *fu* literary genre appeared in the Han Dynasty. It is a type of prose-poem writing, which employed eloquent language to rhapsodize the grandness of the empire and its material and spiritual abundance. Sima Xiangru (?-118 BC) was the best-known *fu* writer of the time. His famous works include *Ai Ershi Fu* (*Rhapsody in Lament of the Second Emperor of Qin*), *Changmen Fu* (*Rhapsody of the Wide Gate*). Most of his *fu* were descriptions of the grandness of imperial hunting expeditions, using lofty language with literary grace.

Zhang Qian, imperial envoy to the Western Regions (138-116 BC)

Zhang Qian (? -114 BC) was a noteworthy diplomat in Chinese history. In 138 BC, he was dispatched as an imperial envoy to Yuezhi, a western nomadic tribe, where he spent 13 difficult years before managing to return to Chang'an in 126 BC. Zhang Qian went on his second trip to the Western Regions in 119 BC, under the order of Han Emperor Wu. Zhang Qian himself went to Wusun (nomadic tribe), and sent other envoys to Dayuan (Ferghana), Anxi (Parthia) and other places. The two diplomatic missions of Zhang Qian strengthened Han ties with minority tribes in the Western Regions, developed friendly relations with the various peoples of Central Asia, and guaranteed the safety of the "Silk Road."

Dunhuang fresco of Zhang Qian's
journey to the Western Regions

The Silk Road

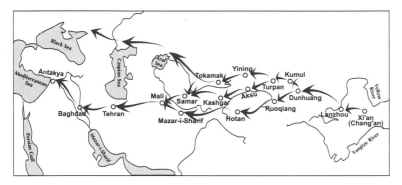

The Silk Road

After Zhang Qian's diplomatic trips to the Western Regions, two routes on land linking Han China to the west were explored. The southern route started from Chang'an, and led to Yuezhi and Anxi through the Hexi Corridor. The northern route went through Dunhuang, Kucha, Kashgar, then over the Pamir Mountains, and finally reached Rome via Anxi. During the following 1,000-year period starting from the 2nd century BC, a great number of Chinese silk and silk products were transported to the west through the Silk Road. An East-West trade system was formed, linking peoples from China, Central Asia, India, Arab regions and Europe. Through these channels, Chinese lacquerware, porcelain, ironware and tea reached far into Europe, while from the west, things like glass, gems, grapes, guavas, walnuts, sesames, cucumbers, garlic and carrots were all introduced to Chinese people. People interested in foreign philosophy and culture also took advantage of the roads. Thus, China's papermaking technologies spread to the west, while Buddhism, Christianity and Islam were brought into China. It was the development of the Silk Road that led to the golden ages of the Han and Tang dynasties.

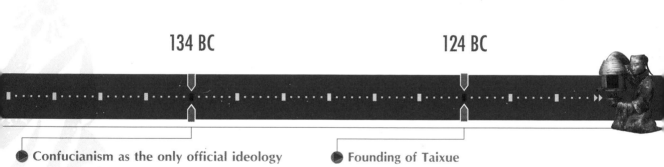

Confucianism as the only official ideology

Founding of Taixue

Portrait of Dong Zhongshu

In 134 BC, Dong Zhongshu (179-104 BC), a Western Han scholar and philosopher, proposed to Emperor Wu that "Confucianism be the only official ideology and all other schools of thought be banned." Absorbing Legalist, Daoist and Yin-Yang elements, Dong redefined Confucianism in the large concept of the "Universe," where "Heaven" is revered as the highest being controlling human fate and ethics is the reflection of heavenly will. In this highly mystified and politicized version of Confucianism, the social and ethical codes of the "three cardinal guides and five constant virtues" were never to be violated. Dong's theory sanctified Confucianism and offered systematic answers to a series of philosophical, political and social questions of that time. As Confucianism helped promote the centralization of power, it gradually became the dominant ideology of China.

In 124 BC, Emperor Wu of Han, adopting the advice of Dong Zhongshu, established a grand school to preach Confucianism. Regarded as the first university in Chinese history, Taixue exercised educational and administrative functions as the highest official school. Students mainly received education in Confucian classics, including *I Ching* (*Book of Changes*), *Shi Jing* (*Book of Odes*), *Shang Shu* (*Classic of History*), *Li Ji* (*Classic of Rites*), along with other Confucian writings. Those who mastered more than one classic text became qualified to fill any vacant official posts. To consolidate the status of Confucianism as the orthodox doctrine, teachings of Confucianism always remained the theme in the imperial university's history of development.

Battle of Mobei, Generals Wei Qing and Huo Qubing

Portrait of Wei Qing

Wei Qing (?-106 BC) and Huo Qubing (140-117 BC) were two great generals during the reign of Han Emperor Wu, whose campaigns against the Xiongnu earned them great acclaim. General Wei was noted for his seven successive campaigns, while General Huo was known for his two complete victories over the Xiongnu in 121 BC, taking control of the Hexi area (now Gansu) and opening the gateway to the Western Regions. In 119 BC, the two generals launched a joint attack on the Xiongnu, and eliminated the enemy at Mobei. The great victories of Wei and Huo drove the Xiongnu tribes out of Han China's territory, and also guaranteed the safety of the Silk Road.

Five-*zhu* Coin

In his fourth currency reform in 118 BC, Han Emperor Wu ordered the minting and circulation of five-*zhu* coins across the country. These coins were round in shape with square hollows in the center, weighing 5 *zhu* (~3.33 g). At first, private mintage was permitted, but soon resulted in currency chaos because of different standards in coinage. In 113 BC, the government imposed a monopoly on mintage, and set up a special institute to monitor coinage. In the following 700 years, five-*zhu* coins were produced in every dynasty, to become the currency with the longest period and largest volume of circulation in Chinese history.

A string of five-*zhu* coins

Iron mold for minting five-*zhu* coins

Yuefu, Chinese folk lyric

Facsimile of *Yuefu* Poetry Collection

Fully developed in the Han Dynasty, *yuefu* was a form of poetry using simple language that told stories of ordinary people. Literally meaning "music bureau," "*yuefu*" originally referred to the government institute in charge of collecting and composing melodies with lyrics that were sung. These lyric poems were thus called "*yuefu* poetry," and included folksongs, poems, and more often, ballads describing everyday life and the pursuit of freedom. Two representative *yuefu* poems were *Ballad of Mulan* and *The Peacock Flies Southeast*.

Sima Qian and his *Records of the Historian* (108-91 BC)

Taichu Calendar

Portrait of Sima Qian

Sima Qian (145-90 BC), the most famed historian in Chinese history, was a native of Xiayang (now Hancheng, Shaanxi). In 108 BC, he was appointed by Han Emperor Wu as Prefect of the Grand Scribes, to compile a set of historical records of China, which became known as *Records of the Historian*. In 99 BC, Sima Qian was castrated and thrown into prison for offending the emperor. Upon his release, Sima Qian lived on to complete his work, around 91 BC. The 130 chapters of the text classified information into five categories: *Benji* (Basic Annals), *Shijia* (Hereditary Houses), *Liezhuan* (Memoirs), *Shu* (Essays), and *Biao* (Chronologies). Recounting the history of China, covering more than 2,000 years from the Yellow Emperor to Han Emperor Wu of his time, the grand historical and biographical work features skillful depiction and concise language in an innovative approach, which has served as a model in Chinese historiography.

Facsimile of *Records of the Historian*

In the early years of the Western Han Dynasty, the inaccurate Qin calendar was still in use. In 104 BC, two astronomers Luoxia Hong and Deng Ping developed a new calendar: the Taichuli. The new calendar stated, there are 365.2502 days in a year, and 29.53086 days in a month. The first month of the year was changed from the 10th to the 1st lunar month. The "24 Solar Terms" were adopted to guide agricultural production. Based on careful research of past astronomical data, the compilers also summarized the solar eclipse periods at 135 months. As the first comprehensively collated calendar in ancient China, the Taichuli was also the most advanced among contemporary calendars in the world. The Taichu Calendar remained in use for 189 years.

Roman statesman and philosopher M.T. Cicero (106-43 BC) originated a systematic account of "Natural Laws," and established the eclectic school of thought.

Zhao Guo and his "furrow-ridge-rotating farming method"

During the rule of Emperor Wu, Zhao Guo (birth and death unknown), an official in charge of collecting grain for armies, invented a "furrow-ridge-rotating farming method" after studying dry farming conditions of northern China. In the new cultivation method, the fields were ploughed with alternating furrows and ridges. Seeds were sowed into the furrows thus being protected from wind and drought. Each year the soil was prepared, and the furrows and ridges were rotated to balance the soil fertility. After seedlings emerged, the soil was fallowed, and the ridges and furrows were made level with each other. Zhao also invented a series of new farm tools, including the *ouli* (plow guided by two men), *louli* (animal-pulled plow), and *louche* (plow combined with sowing device). Together with the newly invented farm tools, farming efficiency was greatly increased with the new tilling methods, where only one man was needed to guide the two-oxen-pulled plow.

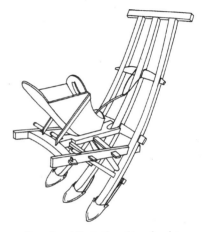

Reproduced illustration of *Louche* plow

The *louche* was invented by a group of artisans under the leadership of Zhao Guo. Placed in a funnel connected to a tube below, seeds automatically dropped when the apparatus was shaken. *Louche* could plow even-spaced furrows, and then sow seeds in them. Because of its farming efficiency, sowing with *louche* became widely adopted in the Han Dynasty.

Eastern Han stone relief of oxen-pulled plowing

The Salt and Iron Conference

Grain storage further systemized

Earliest records of black sunspots

In the Han Dynasty, high-ranking officials and politicians often gathered to discuss political and economic issues. In 81 BC, one such meeting debated the issues of salt and iron. The Legalists represented government officials, while the other side had local government representatives who upheld Confucianism. The debate centered on the state monopoly of salt and iron trade, government price-control measures, and measures against excessive profits of merchants. Issues of national defense, diplomatic relations, crime control, social stability, adopting harsh laws and adherence to moral education were also discussed.

Brick relief with archers and reapers

Grain storage was set up as a national treasury program in the Xia Dynasty. In 54 BC, Emperor Xuan (r. 73-49BC) of the Han Dynasty set up standard price granaries at border prefectures, and adopted a policy of purchasing grains when prices were low and selling when high. The storage system played a positive role in controlling the market, regulating prices, helping the poor during crop failures and preparing against wars. It became a basic system for all Chinese dynasties.

It is recorded in *History of Han Five Elements*: "In the 4th moon of the 1st year of the Yongguang Reign of Emperor Yuan of the Han Dynasty... Black inclined on the side of the sun, big as a pellet." This referred to a black sunspot, as big as a pellet, in an inclining shape, on one side of the sun. The 1st year of the Yongguang reign was 43 BC. The same book also noted: "In the 3rd moon of the 1st year of the Heping Reign..., the sun was yellow, with Black big as a coin found in the center." This sunspot was recorded on May 10, 28 BC. Most scholars believe them to be the earliest records of sunspots in the world.

◎ 73 -71 BC: Spartacus uprising in Rome.
◎ *c*. 57 BC: The ancient state of Silla was founded in Korea

▶ Wang Zhaojun goes beyond the Great Wall   ## ▶ Liu Xiang and Liu Xin

▶ During the reign of Han Emperor Yuan, the Xiongnu split into five separate tribes as a result of power struggles among aristocrats, thus no longer presenting a major threat to the Han Dynasty. In 33 BC, Huhanxie Chanyu (king) from one of the five tribes, visited the Han capital Chang'an to pay homage to the emperor, and requested marriage into the imperial family. Wang Zhaojun or Wang Qiang, a beautiful lady-in-waiting from Zigui (now in Hubei) of the imperial court, requested that the emperor permit her to marry to the king. She not only thus introduced the advanced culture and production skills of the Central Plains region to the Xiongnu, but also brought peace there. From then on, the Xiongnu and the Han Dynasty remained at peace for more than 60 years. The story of Wang Zhaojun is widely known in China, and depicted in many theatrical and literary works.

Portrait of Liu Xiang

Facsimile of *Strategies of the Warring States*

▶ Liu Xiang (77-6 BC) and his son Liu Xin (?-AD 23) were both renowned scholars of the Western Han Dynasty. They were celebrated for their accomplishments in classifying and compiling books, including *Chu Ci* (*Poetry of the South*), *Zhanguo Ce* (*Strategies of the Warring States*), *Shuo Yuan* (*Garden of Tales and Anecdotes*), as well as *Lienü Zhuan* (*Biographies of Exemplary Women*). *Bie Lu* (*Detached Catalogue*), compiled by Liu Xiang, was the earliest classified catalogue of books, and *Qi Lüe* (*Compendium of Books in Seven Categories*) compiled by his son Liu Xin laid the foundation for the bibliographic development in China. Liu Xiang also wrote more than 30 prose poems, while Liu Xin was proficient in mathematics, with his calculation of the ratio of a circle's circumference to its diameter as 3.1457, hence known in China as "Liu Xin Pi."

Zhaojun Goes beyond the Great Wall (detail)

◎ *c*. 37 BC: The ancient Korean State of Koguryo was established.

◎ 27 BC: Gaius Julius Caesar Octavian (Augustus, 63 BC- AD 14) became the first emperor to mark the beginning of the Roman Empire.

2 BC

Introduction of Buddhism into China

In 2 BC, Yi Cun, an imperial envoy of Yuezhi (ancient Central Asian people) arrived in Chang'an, and dictated Buddhist sutras to Jing Lu, a doctorate student. This is generally acknowledged as the first recorded introduction of Buddhism into China. In the Eastern Han Dynasty, Emperor Ming (r. 57-75) sent envoys to the State of Yuezhi to transcribe 42 chapters of Buddhist scriptures, *Sutras of Forty-two Chapters*. The first Buddhist believers in China were high-profile gentry, who interpreted Buddhism using Daoist concepts of moderation, spontaneity, and abstinence from luxurious lifestyles. The Buddha was seen as a counterpart of Laozi, the founder of Daoism. In AD 193, Zuo Rong, a native of Danyang, initiated large-scale construction of Buddhist temples and statues. He also encouraged people to convert to Buddhism by offering exemption from compulsory service. Zuo's efforts led the first wave of Buddhist development in China.

Han Dynasty petroglyphs on Kongwang Mountain, the earliest Buddhist cliffside carvings in China

Yang Xiong wrote *Fa Yan* and *Book of Tai Xuan*

Yang Xiong (53 BC-AD 18) was a philosopher of the Han Dynasty. He first wrote *Fa Yan* (*Words to Live By*) in 13 volumes by emulating the style of *The Analects of Confucius*, with the aim of using the doctrines of propriety and righteousness advocated by Confucius and Mencius to criticize the mystical ideas of that time, thus defending the orthodox ideology of Confucianism. Later, he wrote the divinatory *Book of Taixuan* (*Great Mystery*) by emulating the *Book of Changes*, expounding on relationships between Heaven, Earth and Humans. He stressed that people could achieve the "Way of Heaven" through their own initiative. His theory enriched the ideological systems of traditional Chinese theory of change, thus formulating a knowledge system integrating Confucianism with cosmology.

◎ 18 BC: The ancient Korean State of Paekche was founded.

◎ AD 1 or 4: Jesus Christ, who inspired the Christian religion, was said to have been born.

Wang Mang introduced institutional reforms (AD 8-23)

Lulin and Chimei Uprisings (AD 17-23)

Coins issued by Wang Mang

The last 50 years of the Western Han Dynasty witnessed constant replacements of young emperors, power struggles among imperial in-laws, and successive peasants' uprisings. In AD 8, one such imperial in-law, Wang Mang dethroned the emperor of the Han Dynasty and set himself up as emperor of his short-lived Xin Dynasty. His institutional reforms included nationalization of land, prohibition of selling of servants, state monopoly over liquor industry and salt and ironware trade, as well as taxation over mountains and waters. But these measures only further aggravated the sufferings of the people, and finally led to the Lulin and Chimei uprisings.

Under the rule of Wang Mang, the region around Jingzhou suffered severe drought and many people died of starvation in AD 17. Wang Kuang and Wang Feng organized starving peasants in a revolt and occupied a greenwood mountain area to fight government troops, an event known historically as the "Lulin Army" or "Greenwood Army" uprising. In the following year, the Yellow River changed its course and floodwaters swept the whole nation into chaos. A peasant uprising broke out in Shandong, where famine was most severe. Tens of thousands of peasants assembled and dyed their eyebrows red — hence called the "Chimei" or "Red-eyebrow Army." At the same time, the old Han aristocrats and big landlord families also organized revolts. Under the banner of restoring the Han Dynasty, the rebel forces supported a member of the Liu family as their leader, and restored the Han House after overthrowing Wang's rule.

AD 25 - 220

● As its capital Luoyang was located to the east of the Western Han capital Chang'an, the Han Dynasty founded by Liu Xiu came to be historically called the "Eastern Han Dynasty," lasting from AD 25 until its fall in 220. It witnessed 14 emperors, and its establishment marked the resurgence of the Han Dynasty. However, its stable period lasted less than 80 years, after which the Eastern Han had the same characteristics as the Western Han: most of the emperors becoming puppets due to youth and inexperience, with power controlled by imperial in-laws and eunuchs. The central government also failed to take any measure to restrict the development of local influential and wealthy clans, resulting in regional secessionism and the ultimate downfall of the dynasty. This was followed by four centuries of division and war.

Galloping Horse Overtaking a Flying Swallow, a bronze statue capturing the dynamic moment

Liu Xiu

● Liu Xiu (6-57) was a member of the Western Han imperial family. In the later Wang Mang period, he revolted and joined the Lulin Army, becoming the rebel army leader. In AD 23, he led forces to wipe out Wang Mang's main force at Kunyang (now Yexian Country, Henan), expanding his own influence. He became emperor in AD 25, founding the Eastern Han Dynasty with the capital in Luoyang. He is historically known as "Emperor Guangwu." Liu Xiu suppressed the Chimei Army and wiped out secessionist forces to reunify the whole nation. He reinstated the light tax rates of the early Western Han, organized the troops, released criminals to open up wastelands, and had water conservancy projects built nationwide. These measures led to social stability, economic recovery and population growth in the early Eastern Han Dynasty, to be known as the "Guangwu Resurgence."

○ AD 33: Jesus Christ was said to have been executed by crucifixion, after which his disciples began to spread Christianity.

Nine Chapters on Mathematical Art

Baima (White Horse) Temple

Facsimile of *Nine Chapters on Mathematical Arts*

Nine Chapters on Mathematical Art is an ancient Chinese book on mathematics. It takes the form of a collection of 246 applied questions, with solutions related to production and life. It is divided into nine chapters: *Fangtian, Sumi, Shuaifen, Shaoguang, Shanggong, Junshu, Yingbuzu, Fangcheng*, and *Gougu*. Each problem has a question, an answer and steps for solution. It gives a systematic description of fractional operations, a negative numbers concept, and rules for addition and subtraction of positive and negative numbers, thus marking the formal establishment of the Chinese ancient mathematical system.

In the year 64, Emperor Ming of the Eastern Han sent an envoy to the Western Regions to search for Buddhist scriptures. Three years later, the envoy, together with two eminent Indian monks, used a white horse to convey the Buddhist scriptures and a Buddha statue back to Luoyang. The emperor ordered people to build a temple in the capital city for the monks to live in and to translate the scriptures into Chinese. The temple was named "White Horse" to commemorate the episode. The Baima Temple is thus regarded as "the ancestral Buddhist temple," where the earliest Indian monks visiting China lived, the earliest Sanskrit Buddhist scriptures were kept and the earliest translation site was located, and where China's first monk of Han nationality had his head shaved.

White Horse Temple

◎ 1st-5th centuries: The period of the Guishuang (Kushan) Empire in Central Asia.
◎ 1st-10th centuries: The period of the Kingdom of Aksum in Africa.

Wang Jing harnessed the Yellow River

Ban Chao governed the Western Regions (73-102)

The Yellow River changed course and flooded neighboring areas several times, thus causing social instability during the 1st century's Eastern Han period. In the year 69, the government drafted hundreds of thousand peasants and ordered Wang Jing (c. 30-85), a water conservancy specialist, to harness the river. Wang led the workers in dredging the silted course and building embankments and diversion ditches along the river. When dredging a particular section at Biankou, he created the water-gate control method, and built a number of water-diversion gates every 5 km along the canal to divert water from the Yellow River, so as to regulate the water flow along the river, thus effectively preventing possible breach of dykes.

Ban Chao (32-102) was a general and diplomat of the Eastern Han Dynasty. In the year 73, he led a group of 36 officials to the Western Regions to persuade local states to cut off relations with the Xiongnu, and ally with the Eastern Han. By AD 80, many small states had come over to side with the Eastern Han, but the Xiongnu still launched counteroffensives. With the support of reinforcements and local forces, Ban Chao fought back and quelled the rebellions one after another, establishing a supreme military and administrative stronghold — the Protectorate of the Western Regions. From then on, Ban Chao remained there permanently, governing the region for 31 years, with more than 50 states in the region submitting to the authority of the Eastern Han, thus strengthening the ties between the Western Regions and the Central Plains area and assuring smooth passage along the Silk Road.

Ban Chao's journey to the Western Regions

Publius Cornelius Tacitus (c. 55-120), a Roman historian, wrote the *Histories*, *Annals*, and *The Germania*.

AD 82

AD 83

● Ban Gu and *History of Han*

● Wang Chong and *Lun Heng*

Portrait of Ban Gu

Facsimile of *History of Han*

● Ban Gu (32-92), an Eastern Han historian, was from a historian family. Ban Gu spent more than two decades writing 100 tracts for his *History of Han* and completed the work in AD 82. In this dynastic history book, he detailed an accurate account of the major historical events of nearly 200 years, starting from Emperor Gaozu, founder of the Han Dynasty, to Wang Mang. In geography especially, he not only created a precedent in writing official geographic history, including a style in writing administrative and regional geography, but was also path-breaking in the study of geographic changes and developments as well as frontier geography.

● Philosopher Wang Chong (27-97) wrote 85 essays for his *Discourses Weighed in the Balance* (*Lun Heng*), finishing the book in AD 83 after more than 30 years. He argued that Heaven was an objective physical entity and had no ideology, and that any "correspondence between Heaven and Humans" was sheer nonsense. He thus repudiated the prevailing ideology of the Han Dynasty. He held that the human spirit could not exist if separated from its physical body. Moreover, although accepting Confucius as a sage and not objecting to the moral concepts advocated, he opposed turning Confucian classics into dogmas.

Portrait of Wang Chong

Facsimiles of *Discourses Weighed in the Balance*

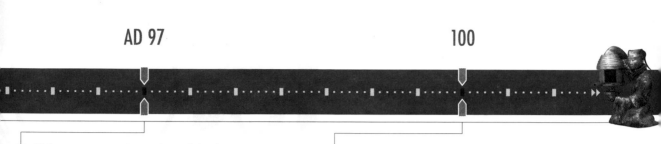

● Chinese envoy Gan Ying visited the Persian Gulf

● Xu Shen and *Explanation and Study of Principles of Composition of Characters*

● Xu Shen (*c.* 58-147) was an Eastern Han economist and scholar. He wrote 15 tracts for *Shuowen Jiezi* (*Explanation and Study of Principles of Composition of Characters*), mainly based on the *xiaozhuan* (small seal) script, but also including the *zhouwen* and the ancient "Six States" scripts used

Facsimile of *Explanation and Study of Principles of Composition of Characters*

during the Qin Dynasty. The characters were arranged according to the order of 540 radicals. Each *zhuan* character was accompanied by meanings, notes and explanations on the composition of the character's form, some including phonetic pronunciations. It was China's earliest and most authoritative dictionary of ancient written characters, contributing enormously to the study of the form, phonetic pronunciation and meaning of ancient Chinese characters and their development.

● Ban Chao, protectorate general of the Western Regions, sent Gan Ying (Birth and death unknown) as his envoy heading a delegation to Daqin (the Roman Empire). The mission set out from Qiuci (today's Kuqa or Kucha in Xinjiang), via Tiaozhi (now in Iraq) and Anxi (now Iran), and reached the Xihai (Western Sea) to the west of Anxi, namely the Persian Gulf. Anxi was a trade depot between the Han Dynasty and the Roman Empire, and monopolized the trade in silk and silk products between the Han and the Romans. Perhaps in fear that a direct trade route between the Han Dynasty and the Daqin would hamper its monopoly, Anxi tried its best to dissuade them from going further. Gan Ying never did reach the Roman Empire, but is recorded in history books as the first Chinese to reach the Persian Gulf.

● Divine Farmer's Classic of Materia Medica

● Cai Lun improved the art of papermaking

● *Shennong Bencao Jing (Divine Farmer's Classic of Materia Medica)* was the first pharmacopoeia in China, compiled during the Eastern Han Dynasty. In three volumes, it records 365 medicines, including 252 herbs, 67 animal parts, and 46 minerals. For each medicine, the localities, properties, collections and benefits were recorded in detail. The book also has an introduction on the synergistic effects of different medicines, as well as preparations for simple formulas. More importantly, many specific medicines were also included in the book, e.g., ephedra as a cure for asthma and rhubarb to release internal heat.

Portrait of Cai Lun

● Cai Lun (?-121), a eunuch in the early 2nd century, was once put in charge of creating useful things for the emperor. At first, he was skilled at making mechanical devices, but later he used tree bark, broken fishing nets, rags and fibrous plants to make fibrous paper, learning from experience of making paper from hemp that started in the Western Han Dynasty. This paper was much better for writing, and had more sources of raw materials, thus changing the old custom of using bamboo and wood slips and silk fabrics for writing on. In the 8th century, China's papermaking technology spread to the Arab world and then further to Europe in the 12th century.

Facsimile of *Divine Farmer's Classic of Materia Medica*

Papermaking process in the Han Dynasty

Zhang Heng invented the seismograph

Reconstruction of Zhang's seismograph

Zhang Heng (78-139) was an eminent astronomer in Eastern Han. In 132, Zhang Heng created the world's earliest seismograph in Luoyang, the Eastern Han capital. The instrument's diameter was 1.94 m, and it was made of bronze, in the shape of a wine vessel. It was based on principles of mechanics. When an earthquake occurred, the instrument body was moved by the quake's longitudinal waves, and the gravity pendulum fell in the direction of the quake, pushing a group of levels in the same direction, so that a ball, coming out of the dragon head outside the instrument, dropped into the mouth of a toad. The sound and direction of the drop divulged the earthquake and its direction. It was so sensitive that it could measure minor earthquakes that could not be felt. It marked a great scientific feat of ancient China.

Zhang Heng was proficient in the calendric science, and wrote his astronomical masterpiece *Ling Xian*. He systematically developed Chinese traditional cosmological theory – the "theory of the universe." His theory argued that the Earth was an ellipse, and the sky an expanded space surrounding the Earth. He used this theory to explain many phenomena, including solar and lunar eclipses. All his conclusions were based on his actual observations. He observed and recorded more than 2,500 stars, and created the world's first armillary sphere (celestial globe) driven by dripping water, which could demonstrate astronomical phenomena with relative accuracy.

◎ Galen (129-200) of ancient Rome systemized anatomical knowledge and Greek medicine, creating the discipline of anthropotomy.

◎ 2nd century: Gaius (c.130-180), Roman jurist, had his *Institutes* published, which is the earliest book on science of law extant in the West.

Birth of Daoism

Persecution of scholars and bureaucrats (166-189)

Daoism (Taoism) is a philosophy indigenous to China. The name derived from the supreme belief in "Dao" (the Way), with Laozi (Laotze) respected as its founder. Its classics are *Daodejing* (*The Book of the Way and Virtue*), and *Zhuangzi* (*Book of Master Zhuang*). It was believed that people could become immortal after practicing Daoist doctrines. Daoism became an independent religion in the 2nd century during the Eastern Han Dynasty. When Eastern Han Emperor Shun (125-144) ruled the country, *Taipingjing* was widely circulated among the people. Later, this evolved into Zhang Ling's (34-156) Wudoumi Sect, which mainly taught people to follow Daoism and treat disease and illness by using magic figures and incantations. When Eastern Han Emperor Ling (168-189) ruled the country, Zhang Jiao founded the Taipingdao Sect, using *Taipingjing* as its classic. It advocated magic figures and incantations, while teaching people to treat illness through meditation.

Yuanshi Tianzun (Celestial Venerable of the Primordial Beginning), one of the highest deities in Daoism

In the second half of the 1st century, the state power of the Eastern Han Dynasty fell into the hands of imperial in-laws, while the influence of eunuchs also increased in the court. This roused discontent among the large landlord families and related scholars and bureaucrats. The three forces used and fought against each other. In 166, the eunuchs falsely accused scholars and officials from influential families of "defaming the court," imprisoning and banning them from holding official posts. In 169 and 176, the eunuchs continued to persecute such officials and even their families. The struggle lasted for more than 20 years. The eunuch clique was completely eliminated in 189.

Zheng Xuan

Cai Yong and Xiping Stone Scriptures

Zheng Xuan (127-200) was a commentator and Confucian scholar in the Han Dynasty. At a young age, Zheng devoted himself to learning of Confucian classics. At the age of 18, for financial reasons, he became a low-ranking official, collecting taxes. Later, Zheng was enrolled into the Imperial College (Taixue), where he first studied the new Confucian texts and later older texts with Ma Rong. Zheng began teaching at the age of 42, with a total of about 10,000 students. In 169, he was thrown into prison during the persecution of scholar-officials by corrupt eunuchs. During his 14-year imprisonment, Zheng devoted himself to the study of Confucian texts, and wrote commentaries on 4 of the 13 Confucian classics: *Book of Odes*, *Ritual of Zhou*, *Yi Li*, and *Classic of Rites*.

Facsimile of *Book of Rites* with Zheng's commentaries

Cai Yong (132-192), a scholar in the late Eastern Han Dynasty, was the personification of the calligraphic theories of the Han Dynasty. In the fourth year of the Xiping Reign (175), Cai Yong and other scholars examined and corrected the written characters of the six books of the Confucian classics, and transcribed them on stone steles and had them carved and erected outside the gate of the Imperial College in Luoyang. There were 46 of them, known as Xiping Stone Scriptures, the earliest officially edited Confucian classics.

A fragment of the Xiping Stone Scriptures

Yellow Turban Army Uprising (184-192)

Han Emperor Xian moved the capital to Xi'an

Large numbers of peasants became refugees after losing their land and livelihood in the late Eastern Han Dynasty; and the "Taipingdao Sect," deeply influenced by Daoism, grew quickly, its followers numbering in hundreds of thousand. They were secretly organized into military units. In 184, Zhang Jiao (?-184), leader of the sect, announced their uprising. They wore yellow turbans, calling themselves "Yellow Turban Army." They swept over the northern and western regions of China in the following 10 years. Although the uprising ultimately failed, the ruling position of the Eastern Han Dynasty became nominal by this time, and the state power split and fell into the hands of local lords.

Luoyang, the capital of the Eastern Han Dynasty, fell into the hands of the warlord Dong Zhuo (132-192) in 190. He not only connived with his troops in plundering the prosperous city for several weeks, but also ordered them to set fire to it when withdrawing. The imperial palace, archives and imperial library of the Han Dynasty were all destroyed. Finally, Dong Zhuo took Emperor Xian (r. 190-220) hostage and fled to Xi'an, forcing millions of the residents to move with him. As a result, the city of Luoyang became desolate and uninhabited.

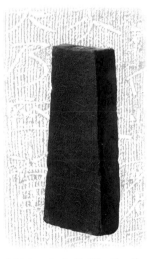

Brick inscribed with "The Blue Sky (Han Dynasty) has perished, the Yellow Sky (rebellion) will soon rise"

▶ Cao Cao's rule in the name of Emperor Xian (196-220)

▶ Cao Cao (155-220) gradually expanded his military strength in the course of suppressing the Yellow Turban Army Uprising. In 196, he coerced Eastern Han Emperor Xian to establish the capital in Xuchang, and usurped power by holding the emperor hostage and acting in his name. After wiping out secessionist forces led by Dong Zhuo and Yuan Shao, he unified the northern part of China. Failing to unify areas south of the Yangtze River, he began to devote his late years to governing northern China and developing local economy. He opened up wasteland for cultivation of food crops, built water conservancy projects, reduced taxes, enlisted talented people, curbed local despotic forces, and strengthened centralized power, leading northern China to economic recovery and growth.

Portrait of Cao Cao

▶ Jian'an Literature

▶ Jian'an Literature refers to literary works from the Jian'an Reign of the late Eastern Han to the early years of the Wei Kingdom. As the literati during this period attentively recorded the social reality of chaos, lamenting miserable lives in the turbulent war years, and expressing longing for national unification and pursuit of a beautiful future, a unique literary style evolved using vigorous, passionate and grievous language. It was called the "Jian'an Ethos." Representative writers of Jian'an Literature include Cao Cao, Cao Pi, Cao Zhi, Kong Rong, and Wang Can. They influenced the literary creations of later generations. The mass of literary works changed to more personal writing. The popular style of poems with five characters per line was introduced as the poetic ideal of the times.

The seven representative figures of Jian'an Literature

● Liu Bei

Liu Bei

● Liu Bei (161-223) earned an initial fame in the course of quelling the Yellow Turban Army Uprising. As his forces grew slowly at first, he could only align himself with different warlords. With the help of two valiant soldiers, Guan Yu and Zhang Fei, and his eminent adviser Zhuge Liang, he gradually expanded his forces. In 208, he united with Sun Quan to inflict a crushing defeat on Cao Cao at Chibi, gradually gaining control of the areas along the upper and middle reaches of the Yangtze River. In 221 Liu Bei proclaimed himself emperor of the Shu Kingdom in Chengdu, Sichuan.

Guan Yu

Guan Yu (162-219) was one of Liu Bei's sworn brothers, and one of the earliest military commanders to follow Liu Bei. He had superb military skills and fought bravely in battles, performing great services for the founding of the Shu Kingdom. He valued personal loyalty and set store by friendship and fidelity, and came to be regarded as the symbol of loyalty and faithfulness by Chinese ancient scholars. He even shared similar fame as that of Confucius. Confucius was called the "scholastic sage," while Guan Yu, the "military sage."

Portrait of Guan Yu

The Battle of Guandu

Hua Tuo

The Battle of Guandu was waged between Cao Cao and powerful warlord Yuan Shao (153-202). In the year 200, Yuan Shao commanded 100,000 crack troops southward to attack Xuchang. Cao Cao, inferior in military strength but well versed in strategy, deployed his troops at Guandu. When Yuan Shao advanced to Guandu, Cao Cao's troops did not meet him head on, but disguised themselves as Yuan's troops, burning Yuan's food and forage in a surprise attack. As a result, Yuan Shao suffered defeat. The Battle of Guandu was an example in which Cao Cao, with an inferior force, defeated Yuan, and destroyed the latter's superior force, thus laying conditions for unifying northern China.

Yuan Shao

Hua Tuo (c. 145-208) was a physician who enjoyed the same fame as Zhang Zhongjing during the Eastern Han Dynasty. He not only had superb skills in internal medicine, gynecology, pediatrics and acupuncture, but was especially adept at surgical operations. He invented a special Chinese anesthesia known as "*mafeisan*," which helped in performing stomach operations on anesthetized patients. Moreover, he also invented a set of exercises called "Five-Animal Exercises," which help to stretch muscles and joints.

Portrait of Hua Tuo

Five-Animal Exercises

Zhang Zhongjing's *Treatise on Cold Pathogenic and Miscellaneous Diseases*

Zhang Zhongjing (150-219) was a physician in the final years of the Eastern Han. In the late 2nd century, typhoid broke out in his native area of Nanyang, killing many people. He delved into medical books and collected many effective prescriptions and herbal remedies. Finally in 204, he completed his *Shanghan Zabing Lun* [*Treatise on Cold Pathogenic and Miscellaneous Diseases*], which was developed by later generations into *On Cold Damage* and *Essential Prescriptions of the Golden Coffer*. In his work, he prepared a series of prescriptions and herbal remedies for clinical treatments, which are still used today. It became the first Chinese work on clinical therapeutics. Moreover, his work also defined a complete set of principles for dialectical therapies. It is regarded as one of the most influential ancient medical classics in Chinese medical history. And its author, Zhang Zhongjing, has thus been honored by later generations as a "medical sage."

Facsimile of *On Cold Damage*

Facsimile of *Essential Prescriptions of the Golden Coffer*

Sun Quan

Portrait of Sun Quan

Sun Quan (182-252), style name Zhongmou, at a young age took control over Jiangdong (southeast of the Yangtze River) with his elder brother Sun Ce, and inherited the territory at 19. In 208, the coalition forces of Sun and Liu Bei defeated Cao Cao in the Chibi Battle. In 229 Sun was proclaimed Emperor of Wu (historically referred to as the Eastern Wu) in Wuchang, and the capital was later moved to Jianye. During his reign, Sun heightened the national power of Eastern Wu, strengthened ties with Yizhou (now Taiwan Province), and set up prefectures and counties in Shanyue (now Vietnam). Sun died of illness in 252.

Zhuge Liang

The Battle of Chibi

Zhuge Liang (181-234) was a legendary figure in Chinese history. He joined Liu Bei's side in 207 after Liu had paid three visits to his humble cottage. He assisted Liu Bei and put into practice his strategic idea of "allying with Sun Quan to resist Cao Cao," which quickly helped Liu Bei become

Zhuge Liang

another secessionist force to rival Cao Cao and Sun Quan, and to finally establish the Kingdom of Shu. This created conditions for a tripartite power balance among the Three Kingdoms. After founding the Shu Kingdom, he brought tribes in southwest China into allegiance to his kingdom and then launched six northern expeditions against the Wei Kingdom in the Central Plains area. He died of illness due to overwork during his last military expedition.

After unifying northern China, Cao Cao tried to conquer the Yangtze River Valley and then unify the whole of China. In 208, he commanded a large army to attack Liu Bei and Sun Quan, confronting the Sun-Liu allied forces at Chibi (in Jiayu territory, today's Hubei). The allied forces took advantage of the vulnerability of Cao Cao's troops who, weakened by an epidemic and poor skills in fighting on water, had linked their boats together with iron chains; they launched an offensive against Cao Cao's troops on both land and water, and burned all his boats, ultimately defeating the 200,000 troops with only a 30,000-strong alliance, laying the foundation for a tripartite power balance among the three kingdoms of Wei, Shu and Wu.

220 - 280

The Three Kingdoms ● Cao Pi (r. 220-226)

● Cao Pi, Cao Cao's second son, eliminated the last emperor of the Han Dynasty and founded the Wei Kingdom in 220. Liu Bei founded the Kingdom of Shu in Chengdu in 221, and Sun Quan became the emperor of the Nanjing-based Wu Kingdom in 229. This signaled the formal beginning of the period of a tripartite power balance among the Three Kingdoms. Previously none of Cao Cao, Liu Bei and Sun Quan dared to replace the emperor of the Han Dynasty though they already had their own spheres of influence and indisputable power in the regions they ruled. As Cao Pi in the north, Liu Bei in southwest China and Sun Quan on the lower reaches of the Yangtze proclaimed themselves emperors one after another within a decade, the Eastern Han Dynasty retreated from the historical stage, and China began the Three Kingdoms Period (220-280).

Cao Pi

● Cao Pi (187-226) was the second son of Cao Cao. After his father's death in 220, he disenthroned Emperor Xian of Han, and proclaimed Emperor of Wei, relocating the capital to Luoyang from Xuchang. During his six-year rule, Cao Pi attached extra importance to education, encouraged reclamation of wild lands, started the court's "nine-grade official ranking system," and further centralized power in his own hands. Cao Pi was also a distinguished man of letters. His *Yan Ge Xing*, completely free from the popular style, became China's earliest and most mature extant seven-character-line poem. He wrote five volumes of *Dian Lun* (*Collected Theses*), and one of the theses, *Lun Wen* (*On Literature*), was considered China's first literary critique. He presented his views on the value and role of literature, literary criticism, the relationship between the writers' temperament and writing style, and differentiation of literary styles.

Wei Wen's trip to Taiwan

Invention of the South Pointing Chariot

The South Pointing Chariot was a geared mechanism used to point out direction in ancient China. The chariot was a two-wheeled vehicle, upon which was a pointing figure connected to the wheels by means of differential gears. The figure atop the chariot would always point in the same direction, hence acting as a non-magnetic compass vehicle. In 235, Ma Jun of the Wei Kingdom constructed one such vehicle, but the manufacturing method was lost. Craftsmen of later generations tried to build replicas of the chariot. In *Song Shi* [*History of the Song Dynasty*], a detailed record of the working mechanism and manufacturing technology of the chariot built by Yan Su [1027] and Wu Deren [1107] served as a vital engineering reference.

In 230, the Wu Kingdom sent General Wei Wen [?-231] and more than 10,000 naval troops to "Yizhou," as Taiwan island was known at the time. They remained in Taiwan for one year. Due to ailments arising from a lack of acclimatization, about 80% to 90% of the officers and men died or became incapacitated. Wei Wen finally returned to the mainland, bringing thousands of native residents from the island with him. From 264 to 280, Shen Ying, chief of Linhai Prefecture of the Wu Kingdom, wrote a book entitled *Linhai Shuitu Zhi* [*Geographic Annals of Linhai*], on the basis of information provided by the returned officers and soldiers as well as the Taiwan residents, providing a detailed social and geographic account of the island.

Replica of a South Pointing Chariot

Wang Bi

Xuanxue metaphysical sect

Wang Bi (226-249) was a philosopher in the Three Kingdoms Period. His philosophical thought could be summed up in one point: "nothing" was the fundamental nature of everything. According to Wang, etiquettes and conventions were tangible in existence with specified names, while what generated benevolence and etiquette was void, intangible and nameless. Therefore, the essence of benevolence and etiquette was to be comprehended by the heart, rather than superficial practice of the conventions. On Confucian scholars' criticism of Laozi's negation of benevolence and etiquette, Wang argued that Laozi was merely emphasizing the significance of "Dao," the formless origin of all benevolence and etiquette. Through his interpretations, Wang integrated Confucianism and Daoism into one, thus laying the metaphysics foundation of the Wei and Jin periods.

Beginning in the 2nd century, Daoist philosophy as advocated by Laozi was rejuvenated in a new form – Xuanxue. Scholars obtained inspirations from the three Daoist classics – the *Book of Changes*, *Laozi* and *Zhuangzi* – to interpret the universe, society and man. However, the seven most-renowned metaphysicians differed in their focus. He Yan and Wang Bi advocated Laozi's idea that "nothing" was the fundamental nature of everything, trying to integrate Daoist metaphysics with Confucian ethics. While Xiang Xiu's ideas resembled those of He and Wang, Ruan Ji and Ji Kang were not hesitant to show disdain for Confucian values and ethics, asserting free-will and liberation of mind advocated by Zhuangzi. Contemptuous of social conventions, they often gathered to enjoy liquor and music, celebrating their return to mature.

Facsimile of He Yan's *Collected Annotations on the Analects*

Ji Kang

Pei Wei, a scholar who realized the social origin of ethics, believed that what lies beneath the surface is not "nothing," but "being," or "social existence." Guo Xiang, last but not least, summarized metaphysics in his assertion that everything in the universe started and evolved on their own, without a common origin. Guo's theory aimed at leading conventional philosophies back to nature, and unifying Confucianism and Daoism.

Seven Sages of the Bamboo Grove

Wang Shuhe and *Canon of the Pulse*

"Seven Sages of the Bamboo Grove" was a collective name given to seven famed scholars during the Wei and Jin periods. The members were Ji Kang, Ruan Ji, Shan Tao, Xiang Xiu, Liu Ling, Wang Rong, and Ruan Xian. The bamboo grove of Shanyang County (now Xiuwu, Henan) witnessed the gatherings of the sages, who enjoyed liquor, personal freedom, spontaneity and celebration of nature. As outstanding figures of the Metaphysical School during the Wei and Jin, the Seven Sages upheld the philosophies of Laozi and Zhuangzi instead of Confucianism, enjoying a free lifestyle unbound by conventional practices. While Shan Tao and Wang Rong became high officials in court, Ji Kang, Ruan Ji and Liu Ling expressed disdain for courtly life, which led to Ji Kang's execution. Their different pursuits of political life eventually fragmented the group.

Facsimile of *Canon of the Pulse*

Wang Shuhe (*c.* 201-280) was a physician during the Wei and Jin periods. He conducted an elaborate study of various medical writings, collecting data about the pulse. After careful selection and compilation, Wang composed *Mai Jing (Canon of the Pulse)*, the earliest systemized text on the subject. With some 100,000 characters in 10 volumes, Wang wrote 98 chapters to describe different properties of the pulse, and for the first time classified 24 types of pulse according to physiological and pathological expressions. For its theoretical profundity and clinical practicality, *Canon of the Pulse* exerted a lasting influence on later physicians.

Seven Sages of the Bamboo Grove (detail)

The Systematic Classic of Acupuncture and Moxibustion

The Systematic Classic of Acupuncture and Moxibustion is the first comprehensive writing on acupuncture in Chinese history, and was composed in 259 by Huangfu Mi (215-282), a physician during the Wei and Jin periods. After studying three acupuncture texts, *Suwen* (*Simple Questions*), *Lingshu* (*Miraculous Pivot*), and *Mingtang's Essentials of Acupuncture Points*, Huangfu selected material on acupuncture to compile his masterpiece. The book contained medical theories and acupuncture practices in 10 volumes (later revised into 12 volumes). Volumes 1 to 6 concentrated on internal organs, channels and collaterals, acupuncture points, diagnostic methods, and pathogenesis. Volumes 7 to 12 covered acupuncture treatments for various illnesses, together with a systemized record of ancient acupuncture therapies. This acupuncture classic served as a valuable source for later physicians.

Facsimile of *Systematic Classic of Acupuncture and Moxibustion*

Liu Hui and Commentaries on the Nine Chapters on Mathematical Art

Nine Chapters on Mathematical Art was a famous mathematical work in ancient China. Compiled in the form of questions and answers, it lacked necessary mathematical proofs. In 263, in his *Commentaries on the Nine Chapters on Mathematical Art*, Liu Hui (c. 225-295) provided solutions to the problems and pointed out mistakes in the book. Liu was credited with the initial establishment of certain mathematical methods. In his work, Liu presented, among many others, an algorithm for the calculation of π or pi, a method to reduce different fractions to a common denominator, a geometrical solution to calculate the area of irregular shapes by dividing and recombining, a solution to calculate the volume of objects, and a solution to calculate the height and distance of faraway objects. Liu Hui's *Commentaries* improved and systemized ancient Chinese mathematics, bestowing a valuable reference for later generations.

265 - 317

Western Jin Dynasty ● Sima Yan founded the Western Jin Dynasty

Sima Yan

● In 265, Sima Yan founded the Jin Dynasty, and reunified China, bringing an end to the Three Kingdoms Period. However, the Western Jin lasted for only 52 years, with four emperors. In its early years, the new dynasty legalized the privileges of influential families, and adopted a rigidly stratified system in honor of distinguished and dominant families of scholar-officials. The subsequent restoration of the enfeoffment system, with blood ties as its link, led to constant turmoil for one third of the period. When aristocrats of tribes from northwest China moved into the Central Plains in large numbers and came into conflict with the Han, the imperial court adopted an indifferent attitude and took no action. As a result, the cavalry of the Xiongnu followed behind the aristocrat migrants and entered the Central Plains. In 311, the Khanate established by Xiongnu aristocrats attacked and occupied Luoyang, capital of the Western Jin Dynasty. The Jin court moved to Chang'an with a new emperor, but Xiongnu armies seized Chang'an in 316, proclaiming the downfall of the Western Jin.

● After the Wei Kingdom was founded, the Sima family usurped all power. In the later period, the emperor of the Wei Kingdom was but a puppet. In 263, Sima Zhao (211-265) wiped out the Shu Kingdom. Two years later, Sima Yan (236-290), son of Sima Zhao, dethroned the emperor of the Wei Kingdom and founded the Western Jin Dynasty. Then, in 280 he destroyed the declining Wu Kingdom, thus bringing an end to the tripartite power balance among the three kingdoms, and reunifying the whole of China.

Western Jin pottery figurines on horseback

▶ The *"menfa"* system of aristocratic politics

▶ War of the Eight Princes (291-306)

▶ *"Menfa"* refers to eminent families of hereditary power and influence that dominated ancient Chinese society over many generations. The system as a form of aristocratic politics was most prevalent in the periods of the Wei Kingdom and the Jin Dynasty, when officials were chosen only from aristocratic *"menfa"* families of scholar-officials. As a result, aristocrats monopolized important posts of the government. In order to preserve their special social position and higher status, the *"menfa"* families of scholar-officials were not allowed to marry families of commoners. There was almost no contact between them. The system led to many social ills, apart from producing a large number of inept aristocrats. It was replaced by the imperial civil examination system in the Sui and Tang dynasties.

Western Jin aristocrats on an expedition

▶ Upon the establishment of the Western Jin Dynasty, 27 princes (kings) of the Sima clan were granted lands by Emperor Sima Yan, governing in a prefectural system. His successor, Emperor Hui was developmentally disabled. Empress Jia Nanfeng, Emperor Hui's wife, plotted a coup in 291 together with Sima Wei, Prince of Chu, only to find the court seized by Sima Liang, Prince of Runan. In the 6th lunar month, Sima Wei killed Sima Liang at the instigation of Empress Jia, who then announced that Sima Wei was acting without imperial orders and executed him. Empress Jia remained in power until her assassination in 300, and the period that followed saw an extremely bloody civil war between the Eight Princes. By its end in 306, the 16-year war brought the devastated country to the brink of collapse. The Sima house suffered a severe reduction of its royal members, who died in the battles against each other. Also, the integrity of the Western Jin Dynasty was greatly threatened by the Xiongnu and Xianbei nomadic peoples, who took the chance to enter China to assist the princes in wars.

Five nomadic tribes and the Sixteen Kingdoms (304-439)

During the turbulent era from late Western Jin Dynasty (304) to the unification of northern China by the Northern Wei in 439, five nomadic tribes established 16 local regimes in northern China. They included the peoples of Xiongnu, Xianbei, Jie, Di and Qiang, who migrated to northern China in the Han Dynasty. The Sixteen Kingdoms they established were as follows: Former Liang, Later Liang, Southern Liang, Western Liang, Northern Liang, Former Zhao, Later Zhao, Former Qin, Later Qin, Western Qin, Former Yan, Later Yan, Southern Yan, Northern Yan, Xia, and Cheng Han. These short-lived kingdoms staged constant wars in the Yellow River region, causing chaos and turbulence in central China for a period of 130 years.

4th century war scene in northern China

Buttocho

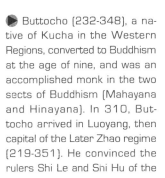

Buttocho

Buttocho (232-348), a native of Kucha in the Western Regions, converted to Buddhism at the age of nine, and was an accomplished monk in the two sects of Buddhism (Mahayana and Hinayana). In 310, Buttocho arrived in Luoyang, then capital of the Later Zhao regime (219-351). He convinced the rulers Shi Le and Shi Hu of the importance of a benevolent government and social justice. With their support, Buttocho committed himself to the spread of Buddhism within China. In his 30-year efforts, Buttocho founded 893 Buddhist temples and preached Buddhist sutras, winning great popularity for Buddhism in China. For his profound knowledge and pious commitment, Buttocho was revered as a Chinese Buddhist master.

312: Constantine I and Licinius promulgated *Edict of Milan*, legalizing Christianity.

317 - 420

● Eastern Jin Dynasty ● Sima Rui founded the Eastern Jin Dynasty

● In 317, Sima Rui re-established the Jin Dynasty, known as the Eastern Jin, in Jian Kang (present-day Nanjing). The Eastern Jin Dynasty maintained its rule for 104 years by relying on the natural barrier of the Yangtze. As there was no major unrest, both culture and the economy developed rapidly in the Yangtze River region. However, there were still many social problems. The development of the "*menfa*" system, in particular, threw state power into the hands of the dominant families of Wang, Xie, Yu and Huan. Too focused on management of their own estates, they made it difficult for the Eastern Jin emperors to make any progress in recovering lost lands in the north. Ultimately, they failed to realize the great feat of reunifying China. Liu Yu, the last prime minister born of a commoner's family, proclaimed himself emperor of the Song (or Liu-Song) in 420, replacing the Eastern Jin and ushering in the period of the Southern Dynasties.

Eastern Jin standing
female figurine

Portrait of Sima Rui

● After the downfall of the Western Jin, surviving members of the Sima family, led by Sima Rui (276-322), crossed the Yangtze River and in 317 founded the new Jin Dynasty in Jiankang. It was historically known as the Eastern Jin, as its capital was located in eastern China. Relying on assistance from Wang Dao and Wang Dun, eminent aristocrats from the north, Sima Rui gained the support of the aristocratic families in regions south of the Yangtze. After political conditions stabilized, he attempted to weaken the power of the Wang families, thus leading to Wang Dun's revolt and ultimate possession of control. Sima Rui died of severe depression in 322.

Ⓒ 320-540: Reign of the Gupta Dynasty in ancient India.

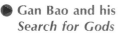

Gan Bao and his *Search for Gods*

Gan Bao (*c.* 283-351) was a historian in the early Eastern Jin Dynasty. His works included *Jin Ji* (*History of Jin*) and *Soushenji* (*Search for Gods*). The latter is a collection of 454 ancient Chinese supernatural stories, mostly about supernatural beings and bizarre events, but some folk tales also being included. These stories are usually short, with simple plots and fantastic premises, greatly influencing the theater and popular literature of later dynasties.

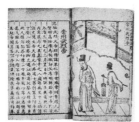

Facsimile of *Search for Gods*

Ge Hong and his *Baopuzi*

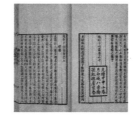

Facsimile of *Baopuzi*

Ge Hong (284-364) wrote many books on immortals and medicine, with *Baopuzi* (Baopuzi was Ge's sobriquet) as his representative work. It gives an account of Daoist theory, how to use plants to treat diseases and how to produce chemical drugs. It reflects Ge Hong's basic ideas on immortality and Confucian teachings. He made outstanding medical achievements. In his *Zhouhou Beiji Fang* (*Handbook on Emergency Prescriptions*), he achieved a relatively complete and accurate description of the danger and infectivity of small pox, the main symptoms of tuberculosis, the characteristics of post-death infection of others, and rabies.

Dao An

Dao An (312-385), with original family name of Wei, became a monk at the age of 12, subsequently studying Buddhism around China, to become an important personage in Chinese Buddhist history. He attached importance to summing up the essence of Buddhist scriptures and their translations, and compiled *Comprehensive Catalogue of Buddhist Scriptures* (*Zongli Zhongjing Mulu*). He initiated the worship of Amitabha, and was the first to publish regulations for monks and nuns, advocating that the family name of all monks should be "Shi" (Chinese initial of Sakyamuni).

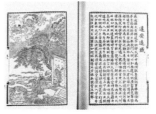

Record about Dao An, in *The Origins of Buddhism*

○ 4th century: Ancient Ghana Kingdom was founded in West Africa.

Wang Xizhi and his Preface to *Orchid Pavilion Collection*

Gu Kaizhi

Preface to *Orchid Pavilion Collection*

Wang Xizhi (321-379), an Eastern Jin calligrapher, came from an aristocratic family, and held the military rank of general of the right-wing army. He initiated a splendid calligraphic style of exquisite writing and varied structure, and further raised the artistic quality of regular and running scripts. In 353, Wang Xizhi, Xie An and 40 other friends had a gathering at the waterside Orchid Pavilion, drinking wine and composing poems. Wang wrote a preface to *Orchid Pavilion Collection*. The 224-character preface he handwrote became a model calligraphic masterpiece in a running style, as well as a superb work of calligraphy.

Gu Kaizhi (345-406), Eastern Jin artist, blended poetry, painting and calligraphy into a single art form. His painting *Look at Wulao Mountain after Snow* was highly acclaimed as a pioneering work. He was skilled in painting figures. He believed that paintings should portray the state of mind and character of the figures therein. Painters should observe the figures and obtain empathy, grasping their inherent nature through thinking in images, then portraying their spirit and state of mind on the basis of formal resemblance — using form to portray spirit. These artistic characteristics were embodied in his representative works *A Female Official's Counsel* and *Ode to the Goddess of the Luo River*, which exerted critical influence on the development of traditional Chinese painting.

A Female Official's Counsel (detail)

○ Mid-4th to 6th centuries: Germanic mass migration.

○ Augustine (354-430), Western Christian philosopher and theologian used neo-Platonist philosophy to expound Christian tenets, and established a "god the father" philosophic system by combining philosophy and theology.

Monk Huiyuan founded the Pure Land Sect

Battle of the Feishui River

Monk Huiyuan

▶ Early in the 5th century, Buddhism witnessed its first surge of development after being introduced into China. The credit for this should go to Huiyuan, an eminent monk in Chinese Buddhist history, who promoted the development of Buddhism in the Yangtze River area. Around 380, Huiyuan founded the largest Buddhist center in the area — the Donglin Temple on Lushan Mountain. In 402, he assembled more than 100 monks to articulate their common desire to be born again in "Western Paradise" — where the Amitabha of the Mahayana (Great Vehicle) lived. This Paradise was a "Pure Land" in the minds of Buddhist followers. The Pure Land Sect of Chinese Buddhism was thus established, with Huiyuan honored as its founder.

▶ In the last years of the 4th century, the Former Qin Kingdom established by the Fu family of the Di ethnicity unified the Yellow River basin areas. Its ruler Fu Jian (338 - 385), in an attempt to reunify a divided China, sought to wipe out the Eastern Jin Dynasty, which had been

Portrait of Xie An

content to control the regions south of the Yangtze River. In 383, he sent more than 800,000 troops southward, and the Eastern Jin dispatched Xie An and Xie Xuan with 80,000 crack troops to face them. The two sides agreed to fight a decisive battle on the western banks of the Feishui River. Fu Jian wanted to intercept the Jin troops when they crossed the river, and decided to retreat first. Unexpectedly, the Former Qin troops, with no will to fight, became discouraged upon retreating. The Jin troops took advantage of the situation to launch an offensive, their troops dealing a crushing defeat on the Former Qin troops, and Fu Jian fled back north in panic. The Battle of the Feishui River ended with a victory in which the Eastern Jin Dynasty used fewer troops to defeat the much stronger Former Qin troops, and became of great significance in safeguarding the stability and prosperity of the southern regions.

◎ 4th-7th centuries: Yamato Period in Japan.

386 - 581

▶ **Northern Dynasties**   ▶ *Northern Wei Dynasty (386-534)*

▶ In 386, Xianbei, a northern nomadic people, established the Northern Wei Dynasty. After seating its capital in Pingcheng (now Datong, Shanxi) in 398, Northern Wei began the annexation of surrounding small kingdoms, and unified north China in 439, posing against the Southern Dynasty that had replaced the Eastern Jin in 420. Northern Wei split into Eastern and Western Wei in 534, followed by Northern Qi and Northern Zhou. This turbulent era is referred to in Chinese history as the Northern Dynasties.

Pottery warriors on horseback

Minority people in northern China working in fields during the Northern Dynasties

▶ In 493, the Northern Wei Dynasty moved its capital to Luoyang, and used political means to force the people to adopt Han family names, speak Chinese, wear Han-style clothes, marry Han women, and follow Han folklore and customs. The Northern Wei rulers also promoted Buddhism by chiseling grottoes, building Buddhist temples, and personally preaching Buddhist scriptures.

Northern Dynasties	
Northern Wei	386 - 534
Eastern Wei	534 - 550
Northern Qi	550 - 577
Western Wei	535 - 556
Northern Zhou	557 - 581

◎ 392: Roman Emperor Theodosius I proclaimed Christianity as the national religion.
◎ 395: Roman Empire was split into the Eastern and Western empires.

Monk Faxian's western pilgrimage (399-412)

Portrait of Faxian

▶ Faxian (334-420) was a monk of the Eastern Jin Dynasty. In 399, he went to India to study Buddhist doctrines and Sanskrit, due to the lack of Buddhist discipline at home. In 412 Faxian brought written scriptures back to China, via the sea route. Faxian's *Pilgrimage to the Land of Buddhism* (*Foguo Ji*), based on his travels and observations, has become an important historical document for the study of Buddhism, history, culture and geography of the ancient states in the Western Regions and India.

Kumarajiva translated Buddhist texts in China (401-413)

▶ Kumarajiva was an Indian monk, born in Qiuci (now Kuqa or Kucha in Xinjiang) in 343. He followed his mother into monasticism at the age of seven, and studied Theravada (Little Vehicle) and Mahayana (Great Vehicle). He arrived in Chang'an, China, in 402, and was named "State Tutor" by the ruler of the Later Qin in 405. He spread Buddhism in China for more than 10 years, and always had large audiences. He set up a translation office in the Xiaoyao Garden, where he translated 384 volumes of 74 scriptures.

Sculpture of Kumarajiva

Tao Yuanming and his *Peach Blossom Spring*

Portrait of
Tao Yuanming

▶ Tao Yuanming (365-427) was an Eastern Jin poet. Obsessed with drinking and reading, he initiated a new style of idyllic poetry, with idyllic life as its theme. *Peach Blossom Spring* is a prose work written by Tao Yuanming, with a poem appended. The work describes the migrants of the pre-Qin period who lived a secluded life of peace in the mountains to escape the chaos of war, "breeding silkworms and reeling silk in spring, and paying no taxes to the court in the harvesting season of autumn." It reflects the author's yearning for a peaceful and natural way of life.

420 - 589

▶ In 420, a new dynasty called the Song established by the Liu family replaced the Eastern Jin. It became historically known as the "Liu-Song Dynasty." In the 170 years since the beginning of the Liu-Song, there were four dynasties, one after another. This historical period is called the "Southern Dynasties." The Liu-Song Dynasty and its successor, the Qi Dynasty, were both toppled by aristocratic families. The third among the Southern Dynasties was the Liang, which represented the sole "golden age" during the Southern period. The development of commerce and trade at this time accelerated the collapse of the "*menfa*" aristocratic politics based on the feudal plantation economy. The Liang was replaced by the Chen Dynasty, which was overthrown by the Sui Dynasty from the north, in 589.

Portrait of Liu Yu

▶ Liu Yu (363-422) was the founder of the Song Dynasty, in the Southern Dynasties period. After joining the Eastern Jin army in his youth, Liu later became an important general leading the Beifu Army, an elite force of the court. In 404, he eliminated the usurper Heng Xuan and restored the Jin emperor, who became but a puppet in his hands. After rooting out the officials against him in the court, Liu led his armies north to conquer the Southern Yan (of the Xianbei people) and the Later Qin (of the Qiang people). In 420, Liu proclaimed himself Emperor of the Song Dynasty, and took various measures to develop national power. He abrogated harsh laws, rectified malpractices in court, placed emphasis on thrift, suppressed powerful local lords, and distributed relief among the people. Under his leadership, southern China saw a period of economic and cultural development.

Combat scene of cavalry and infantry

Southern Dynasties	
Song	420 - 479
Qi	479 - 502
Liang	502 - 557
Chen	557 - 589

Xie Lingyun

Xie Lingyun

▶ Xie Lingyun (385-433), a poet of the Southern Dynasties, held several official posts, but never fulfilled his administrative duties. He visited scenic places in the day and drank wine at night. His landscape poetry constituted a unique school in ancient China's history of literature, portraying natural sights, famous scenery and historic relics in China's southern regions. His school is characterized by the use of a fresh and serene style to convey the Daoist view of nature, and the idea of harmonious coexistence between people and nature.

Liu Yiqing's *New Collection of Anecdotes of Famous Personages*

▶ Liu Yiqing (403-444) was a scholar of the Southern Dynasties. His *New Collection of Anecdotes of Famous Personages* (*Shi Shuo Xin Yu*) was composed of more than 1,000 short stories that are divided into 36 categories, such as moral conducts, dialogues and speeches, political affairs and literature, to reflect the thinking, words and deeds, and lives of literati and the upper strata between the second and fifth centuries. The records are very rich and realistic. Many of the anecdotes and literary allusions in the book were used and quoted by writers of later generations.

Facsimile of *New Collection of Anecdotes of Famous Personages*

Parallel prose

▶ Parallel prose was a new literary form that emerged around the third century, mainly characterized by antithesis in sentence structures and syntactical functions and meaning of characters, with the lines (or sentences) usually alternating between the use of four and six characters. As the lines were paired much like two horses walking neck and neck, this style of writing is called "*pian*" in Chinese, a character that is composed of a left radical that means "horse," and a right part that means "abreast." Representative writers of parallel prose were Bao Zhao (414-466) and Jiang Yan (444-505). This writing style exerted enormous influence on literature and poetry of later generations. Its weakness was its excessive pursuit of structural symmetry, hampering conveying of ideological substances.

453   485

Yungang Grottoes (453-494)   Equal field system

The construction of the Yungang Grottoes in Datong, Shanxi Province, was started in 453, and largely completed by 494. They exemplify Chinese Buddhist grotto art of the 5th and 6th centuries. There are 53 grottoes extant, with 51,000 rock-carved statues, the tallest 17 meters in height, and the smallest only several centimeters. The Buddhist sculptures of warriors and flying apsaras are vivid in imagery, and the carvings on the pagoda columns are exquisite, comprising Buddha figures, coiled dragons, lions, tigers and plant designs. The grotto carvings blended traditional Chinese artistic styles, while assimilating and drawing on the Buddhist Gandhara art from India.

Northern Wei pottery oxcart

In the early Northern Wei Dynasty, land was laid to waste due to long years of wars, seriously affecting tax collection. The government promulgated the "equal field system" edict in 485, by which it nationalized all land, with individuals only entitled to the right of use. Every male at and above the age of 15 was given 40 *mu* (15 *mu* = 1 ha), while each female was given half of this. Slaves or servants enjoyed the same treatment. Land was also given on the basis of the number of draft animals. Sale of the land provided was not permitted. The land had to be returned to the government once users were too old to cultivate it or died. Wasteland was reclaimed after the introduction of the equal field system. This guaranteed stable taxation for the government, and helped to break the control of local society by wealthy families. After cultivators were placed directly under the government, administrative orders were able to reach every family and household.

Buddha statues at the Yungang Grottoes

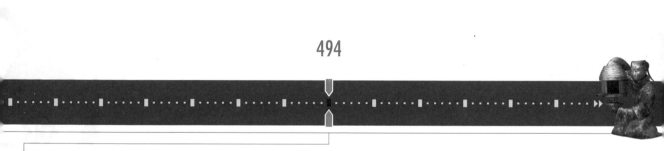
Northern Wei Emperor Xiaowen and his reforms ● Longmen Grottoes

● Emperor Xiaowen (467-499), named Tuoba Hong, was an able emperor of the Northern Wei Dynasty. Upon his succession to the throne in 471, he carried out a series of political and economic reforms. In 494, Luoyang was made the new capital, replacing Pingcheng (now Datong, Shanxi), and large-scale sinicization began. The emperor ordered the population to speak the Chinese language, wear Han clothes, change Xianbei surnames into Han names, and encouraged intermarriage between Xianbei nobles and Han official families. He also adopted the Han bureaucratic establishment, legal system, ritual practices, and law codes. The measures taken by Emperor Xiaowen hastened the sinicization of the Xianbei people, and helped national integration in northern China.

Sculpture of Vairocana at Fengxian Temple

● Located south of Luoyang, Henan Province, the Longmen Grottoes were first constructed in 494, and chiseling continued for 1,000 years. But most of the Buddhist sculptures were from the Northern Wei and Tang dynasties. Now there are more than 2,100 caves and shrines, 43 pagodas, 3,860 inscriptions, and over 100,000 Buddhist images. The images carved are mostly of Buddha, Bodhisattva, disciples, and other Buddhist figures. There are also inscriptions of pious followers and Buddhist tales. In addition to its religious collection, Longmen Grottoes also offer valuable records on ancient paintings, calligraphy, music, costumes, medicine, architecture, and communication. Along with the Mogao and Yungang Grottoes, the Longmen Grottoes are one of China's three most famous ancient sculptural sites.

Emperor Xiaowen of Northern Wei paying homage to Buddha

◎ 476: The Western Roman Empire collapsed.

▶ Zu Chongzhi's pi

Portrait of Zu Chongzhi

▶ Zu Chongzhi (429-500) was a scientist during the period of the Liu-Song and Qi dynasties. His greatest achievements were in the field of mathematics. He successfully calculated pi to the precision of 3.1415926 and 3.1415927, and also obtained two fractional approximations: a close approximation of 355/113, and a rough approximation of 22/7. He achieved the result by segmenting a circle into a polygon of 24,576 sides, and thus became the first person in the world to calculate the accurate value of pi to 7 decimals.

▶ Tao Hongjing and *Commentary on Shen Nong*

▶ Tao Hongjing (456-536) was a Daoist monk of the Southern Dynasties. He was obsessed with the Daoist art of maintaining good health and method of keeping fit through physical and breathing exercises. He spent his whole life in classifying and compiling Daoist classics and books on Daoist ways of health preservation. He revised the ancient medical book *Shen Nong Bencao Jing* (*Shen Nong's Herbal Classic*) and compiled the book *Bencao Jing Jizhu* (*Commentary on Shen Nong*) in 500, describing 730 varieties of medicinal substances including their names, places of origin, properties, applications, and methods of their preparation and preservation.

▶ Liu Xie and *The Literary Mind and Carving of the Dragon*

Facsimile of *The Literary Mind and Carving of the Dragon*

▶ Liu Xie (466-538) wrote *The Literary Mind and Carving of the Dragon* (*Wen Xin Diao Long*) in 502 — China's first systematic theoretical work in literary criticism. The book deals with literati and literary creations, the imaginative power of the arts, the creative style of literary works, basic theories of literary appreciation and criticism, as well as literary form and origin. The book stresses that literature has its own characteristics, that literary works should be "new and fresh every day." He placed equal emphasis on form and quality.

◎ 493-555: Germanic Ostrogoth Kingdom, or East Goth Kingdom.
◎ Late 5th to late 10th centuries: The Frankish Kingdom.

Fan Zhen and *Shen Mie Lun* (*On the Extinction of Spirit*)

Fan Zhen

▶ The atheist Fan Zhen (*c.* 450-515) rose when Buddhism was prevalent during the Qi and Liang periods of the Southern Dynasties. He wrote *On the Extinction of Spirit*, in which he said that, the spirit and the form of humans was a unity of mutual integrity. Without form, there was no "spirit." He denounced the Buddhist theory of retribution as sheer nonsense. In the Liang period, Emperor Wu, himself a faithful believer in Buddhism, brought more than 60 princes, dukes, influential officials and monks together to publish more than 70 articles to refute him, but Fan Zhen never yielded.

Li Daoyuan and *Commentary on Waterways*

▶ Li Daoyuan (466-527) was a geographer of the Northern Wei Dynasty. Using the ancient geographical book *Waterways* (*Shuijing*) as a basis, he compiled *Commentary on Waterways* (*Shuijing Zhu*) in 40 volumes. The book annotates the alignments and basins of more than 1,250 large and small rivers, and describes the mountains, lakes, counties, cities, soils, vegetations, climates, hydrology, society, economies, and folk customs in the regions they flow through. It is China's first comprehensive geographical work focused on describing waterways.

Facsimile of *Commentary on Waterways*

Bodhidharma founded the Chan (Zen) Sect of Buddhism

Bodhidharma

▶ A monk named Bodhidharma (?-536) from South India came to China in the 6th century and founded a new sect of Buddhism in China — Chan or Zen. Chan means "meditation," a type of Buddhist cultivation. It does not believe in the use of written script, nor is there need to chant scriptures and pray before images of the Buddha or perform any complicated religious services. It holds that, as long as one persists in believing that one has the nature of the Buddha, one will attain the complete intuitive illumination of one's nature of the Buddha through meditation after a certain amount of religious experience.

▶ Xiao Tong and Zhao Ming Collection

▶ Xiao Tong (501-531) was the son of Xiao Yan, Emperor Wu of the Liang during the Southern Dynasties period. Due to his early death, he never succeeded to the throne, but he compiled *Zhao Ming Collection* — China's earliest extant collection of literary works. The collection contains more than 700 pieces selected from 130 writers of the previous 700 years, including prose, poems and essays. It was considered a must for literary research by later generations.

Facsimile of *Zhao Ming Collection*

▶ Memoirs of Eminent Monks

▶ *Memoirs of Eminent Monks* is a compilation of biographies of important monks in China, from the introduction of Buddhism in the early Eastern Han Dynasty up to 519 in the Liang Dynasty. The book was compiled around 530 by Huijiao (497-554), a Liang monk. The 13-volume book has records of 257 accomplished monks, with another 200 figures also mentioned. The stories are classified into 10 categories: translation, interpretation, divinity, meditation, discipline, anatta, sutra chanting, blessings, masters, and preaching. *Memoirs of Eminent Monks* is the first systemized biographical writing on Buddhist monks in China, as well as a valuable source for historical and literary studies of the period.

▶ Jia Sixie's *Qi Min Yao Shu* (*Important Arts for People's Welfare*)

Facsimile of *Important Arts for People's Welfare*

▶ Jia Sixie, an agricultural scientist of the late Northern Wei Dynasty, devoted his life to the study of agricultural production technology. From 533-534, he wrote *Qi Min Yao Shu* (*Important Arts for People's Welfare*), after collecting documents and peasant proverbs, paying visits to experienced cultivators and conducting field experiments. The book was a systematic summary of experience in farm production and stock breeding in the Yellow and Huaihe river regions before the 6th century.

© 529: Justinian the Great (r. 526-565), Byzantine emperor, issued an edict to compile the *Corpus Juris Civilis* (*Body of Civil Law*), known as the *Justinian Code*.

581 - 618

Portrait of
Emperor Wen of Sui

▶ Sui Dynasty ▶ Yang Jian, Sui Emperor Wen (r. 581- 604)

▶ The Sui Dynasty was established in 581, and destroyed in 618, with two emperors over 38 years. In this short period, it reunified China, expanded its territorial area, and adopted a series of measures to achieve social stability and economic development. Its system of three councils and six ministries and imperial civil examination system influenced China for more than 1,300 years. After Emperor Yang succeeded to the throne, the governing environment fell into disarray. Moreover, the emperor used too much labor and material resources on the construction of the Eastern capital, Grand Canal, Great Wall and royal roads, as well as on his pleasure tours around the country and constant wars; thus driving the people into dire poverty and causing grievances among them. This led to the downfall of the Sui Dynasty.

▶ China was politically divided for nearly 300 years, from the late Eastern Han to the Chen Dynasty (557-589) in south China. This state of affairs was brought to an end by Yang Jian (541-604), from an aristocratic family. In 580, by assisting the emperor of the Northern Zhou Dynasty (557-581) in north China in the capacity of prime minister, and as a relative of the emperor's wife, he established the Sui Dynasty in 581, by killing the emperor of the Northern Zhou and proclaiming himself the Sui emperor. He took the throne for 24 years. Under his rule, the Sui eliminated the Later Liang and Chen dynasties in the south one after another, to put an end to the prolonged situation of division, thus reunifying China. In 604, he was killed by his son Yang Guang.

Sui Dynasty figurine
of a civil officer

○ Mohammed (*c*. 570-632) founded Islam.

System of Three Councils and Six Ministries

The system of three councils and six ministers, initiated by Emperor Wen, was the central bureaucratic system of the Sui Dynasty. The three councils were Zhong Shu Sheng, Men Xia Sheng and Shang Shu Sheng. They were considered the supreme administration, and their chiefs were prime ministers who together discussed state affairs. Under Shang Shu Sheng were the six ministries of personnel, population and taxation, education and protocol, war, justice, and public works. Their functions were appointment and dismissal of officials, population management and tax collection, education and ceremonies, military affairs and national defense, justice and prisons, and engineering works. Their chiefs were all called Shang Shu or ministers. Generally speaking, Zhong Shu Sheng was a decision-making body, Men Xia Sheng was a deliberative body, and Shang Shu Sheng was an executive body, but they undertook joint responsibilities under the emperor. Its establishment marked important reform of China's ancient political system and officialdom. It began to separate the private affairs of the emperors from state affairs. There was a distinct division of work between the different departments handling state affairs, which helped to improve administrative efficiency.

The imperial civil examination

Attending the imperial civil examination in the Song Dynasty

Emperor Wen of the Sui Dynasty initiated imperial examinations in 587, to select talent from among the common people. Those who passed the examination were given official posts. The examinations developed into a system. The system of using examinations to select talented people for official posts came to be known as the "imperial civil examination." While discovering talent for the government, the examination system also provided a channel for intellectuals from commoner families to seek government posts. From the Sui onwards, all dynasties adopted this system to select talent, with changes only in content and methods. It was abolished in 1905, before the fall of the Qing Dynasty.

► Li Chun built Zhaozhou Bridge (595-605)   ► Yang Guang, Sui Emperor Yang (r. 604-618)

► Li Chun was a bridge-building master of the Sui Dynasty. He built the well-known Zhaozhou Bridge in Hebei, between 595 and 605. It had a net span of 37.02 m, a rise of 7.23 m and a width of 9 m. The central arch is made of 28 thin, curved limestone slabs and has two smaller spandrel arches each at the two ends (their net spans, 2.85 m and 3.81 m), which were used to reduce the dead weight of the bridge body and increase the volume of discharged floodwaters. It is the earliest extant open-spandrel segmental arch stone bridge, with the largest span in the world.

Sui Emperor Yang's cruise

► Yang Guang (569-618), the second Sui emperor, was the second son of Yang Jian, the dynasty's founding emperor. Before he succeeded to the throne, he brought false charges against the empress and crown prince, and in 604 killed his father to establish himself as the next emperor. After he succeeded to the throne, he lived extremely extravagantly, misused the people's financial resources, and drafted millions of peasants to toil to build a canal linking the northern and southern parts of China, to make it easier for him to tour the lower reaches of the Yangtze River. Then, he drafted soldiers for successive three years to attack the Koryo Kingdom on the Korean peninsula. Moreover, he built Luoyang despite dwindling national financial resources. All this threw the country into turbulence, with frequent peasant uprisings. In the end, he was hanged by his generals during a tour, and the Sui Dynasty collapsed.

Zhaozhou Bridge

Sui Canal under construction (605-610)

Peasants' uprisings in the late Sui Dynasty (613-617)

Emperor Yang of the Sui Dynasty spent six years opening the 2,000km-long canal from Zhuojun (now Beijing) in the north to Yuhang (now Hangzhou, Zhejiang) in the south. Some of the sections had been dug earlier, and were renovated or improved by deepening and adding sluice gates. In 605, his second reign year, he began to dig the Tongji Canal from Luoyang southward to Shanyang (today's Huai'an, Jiangsu). In 608, he opened the Yongji Canal from Luoyang northward to Zhuojun. Two years later, he opened the Jiangnan Canal from Jingkou (now Zhenjiang, Jiangsu) southward to Yuhang. The projects connected five river systems, including the Yellow, Huaihe and Yangtze rivers.

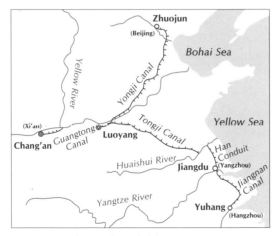

The Grand Canal of the Sui Dynasty

During his reign, Emperor Yang of Sui became committed to many labor-consuming construction projects, and ordered several military expeditions to expand territory. His tyrannical rule, together with frequent natural disasters of floods and drought, left the country bankrupt and the people in revolt. In 613, a peasant force in Shandong launched a rebellion, soon joined by millions of people around the country. Among the local forces, the Wagang Army led by Zhai Rang (?-617), and the armies of Dou Jiande (573-621) and Du Fuwei (596-624) posed the greatest threat. From 613 to 617, these forces ventured into large areas of Shanxi and Hebei to the north, Lingnan to the south, Shandong, Jiangsu and Zhejiang to the east, and the Hexi Corridor to the west. Sui Dynasty rule reached the edge of collapse.

© 606-647: The reign of Harsha Vardhana in India.

618 - 907

Tang Dynasty

Peasant uprisings arose one after another in the late Sui Dynasty. In 617, Li Yuan in Taiyuan rose against the Sui, and captured Chang'an in the following year, establishing the Tang Dynasty. After his son Li Shimin succeeded to the throne, the Tang Dynasty developed quickly, both economically and militarily, bringing the country into a period of brilliance, known in Chinese history as the "Great Reign of Zhenguan." Later, Empress Wu Zetian and Emperor Xuanzong also made great administrative achievements that culminated into the "Great Prosperity of the Kaiyuan Years," during Emperor Xuanzong's reign. After the armed rebellion led by An Lushan and Shi Siming in 755, the Tang began to decline. The "Huang Chao Uprising" in 874 brought the Tang Dynasty to collapse. In 907 it was finally overthrown by the Later Liang Dynasty. The Tang Dynasty had 20 emperors and lasted 290 years.

Layout of Chang'an City

Chang'an, capital city of the Tang Dynasty

The Tang Dynasty during its heyday was very open, liberal and a melting pot for all cultures. Its capital city Chang'an was a good example of the prosperous civilization of that period. Chang'an, first built in 582, with a city wall of 35 km, was the most prosperous city in China, an economic and cultural center of Asia, as well as an international metropolis in the medieval ages. The entire city consisted of the outer city, imperial city and palace. The outer and imperial cities were divided into 108 blocks by orderly streets. The central south-north artery road was 155 m wide. In Chang'an, one could see diverse peoples wearing various folk costumes, foreign merchants and overseas students. The Tang government even set up special reception offices to provide convenient services to new international residents.

Tang Dynasty
figurine of a lady

© 622: Mohamed taught Islam in Mecca, where he was driven out by people; he then led his disciples to Medina.

Li Shimin took power after the Incident at Xuanwu Gate

Great Reign of Zhenguan

Portrait of Li Shimin

Li Shimin (599-649), the second son of Li Yuan, took advantage of the peasant rebellions and convinced his father to rise against Sui rule in Taiyuan. In the ensuing battles, Li displayed his talent for political and military maneuvers, playing a vital role in the capture of the Sui capital Chang'an and the establishment of the Tang Dynasty. Following the tradition of "eldest son as crown prince," Li Yuan made Li Jiancheng his heir, who then saw Li Shimin as a thorn in his side. The crown prince devised multiple assassination plots against his brother, but failed each time. Then in 626 at Xuanwu Gate, Li Shimin staged a coup and killed his brother, forcing his father to make him crown prince. After Li Shimin ascended the throne, he changed the era's title to "Zhenguan." In his hands, the Tang Dynasty enjoyed its first period of prosperity, known as the "Great Reign of Zhenguan."

During his 23-year reign from 627 to 649, Li Shimin, Tang Emperor Taizong, provided an exemplary model for later emperors in Chinese history. Learning from the downfall of the Sui Dynasty, he adopted a series of wise policies. In the court, he promoted able officials, and encouraged the free airing of views. He systemized the legal system, improved the imperial examination system, and sought better relations with other nationalities. To develop the national economy, he adopted favorable policies to encourage agricultural production. Taxes were reduced, and thrift was emphasized. His reign is considered in Chinese history as a great period of national prosperity.

Tang Dynasty Women

Xuanzang's journey to the west seeking scriptures (627-645)

Envoys to the Tang

Xuanzang

The original family name of Xuanzang (596-664) was Chen. He became a monk at the age of 13. In 627, he left Chang'an and went through the Yumen Pass to India. In 631, he arrived at the Nalanda Temple in India, where he stayed for five years studying Buddhist teachings. Afterwards, he traveled to all the renowned Buddhist centers in India, visiting famed Buddhist holy lands on the Ganges River and meeting many eminent monks. He returned to Chang'an in 645, and devoted his remaining years to the translation of Buddhist scriptures. He translated a total of 75 Buddhist scriptures and writings in 1,335 volumes. He also wrote *Records on the Western Regions of the Great Tang Empire*, on the basis of his experiences on the journey, providing important data for the study of the ancient histories and geography of South and Central Asia.

The Tang Dynasty's booming economy, prosperous culture and complete social systems attracted those from neighboring Japan and the Korean Peninsula, who sent many students to China. For example, Japan sent 19 groups, with over 100 students (or envoys to the Tang) on each group, to China. Silla on the Korean Peninsula sent more students to China than any other country, with nearly 200 of them being on long-term stay. Most of the international students were organized to study the Chinese classics, and Tang laws and regulations in the Imperial Academy. They usually studied for over 10 years, sometimes for as many as 20 or 30 years. Some even stayed to work as officials in China. Overseas students enjoyed high social status and reputation when they returned home. They played a great role in introducing China's philosophy, political system, literature and arts, music and dance, astronomy and mathematics, medicine, architecture, costumes and customs to their countries, which became greatly influenced by China.

632: Mohamed led his army to capture Mecca and founded the Islamic Empire, known as the Arab Empire in the West, but as "Dashi" and "Tianfang" in China.

▶ Christianity introduced into China

▶ In its early years, the Tang Dynasty adopted an attitude of tolerance towards all religions and cultures, and Nestorianism — the Nestorian school of Christianity, very popular in the Persian region — was introduced into China at that time. In 635, the first Christian missionary, Bishop Alopen of the Nestorian Church, came to Chang'an along the Silk Road, and the emperor permitted him to stay in Chang'an to translate the Bible and do missionary work in various parts of China. In 845, the Tang Dynasty issued a ban on Buddhism, which also affected Nestorianism and its spread.

Rubbing from a stone inscription recording Nestorianism's spread in China

▶ Princess Wencheng and Songtsam Gambo

▶ In 641, Tang Emperor Taizong ordained the marriage of Princess Wencheng, a daughter of the imperial family, to Songtsam Gambo, King of Tubo (now Tibet). During her stay in Tibet, with her extraordinary political genius she assisted Songtsam Gambo in governing Tubo and preserving peace between the Tang Dynasty and the Tubo, thus winning the respect of the Tibetan people. When she first went to Tibet, she brought many literati, musicians and agricultural technicians, as well as large quantities of production tools, medical instruments, and ancient books and records. Later, she again introduced the technologies of rearing silkworm, winemaking and papermaking to Tibet. As a result, both the culture and economy extensively developed in the region.

▶ Wei Zheng

Portrait of Wei Zheng

▶ After his succession to the throne, Li Shimin employed people of virtue and talent and accepted good advice from all sides. The friendship between the emperor and Minister Wei Zheng was an example. Wei Zheng (580-643) initially assisted crown prince Li Jiancheng, and dared to speak candidly, which Li Shimin valued. So he promoted Wei Zheng to the post of imperial counselor. Wei Zheng assisted the emperor with his heart and soul, and often voiced outspoken criticism before Li Shimin, without considering the consequences. He told the emperor: "Water can carry a boat, but also overturn it."

◎ 645: Emperor Kotoku of Japan took "Taika" as his reign title, and began using the Chinese way of numbering the years of reign and following Chinese methods to reorganize the central government. This came to be known historically as the "Taika Reforms."

Islam introduced into China   ### Sun Simiao   ### *Comments on Laws of the Tang Dynasty*

On 25 August 651, the first diplomatic mission of the Arab Empire arrived in Chang'an. They paid a formal visit to the Tang Emperor, and gave him an account of the religious beliefs and customs of their countries. Most historians regard the visit of the mission to China as marking the formal introduction of Islam in China. During the Tang Dynasty, large numbers of Arabs and Persians came to China through the Silk Road. They intermarried with Chinese people. They could even take imperial civil examinations for government posts, while still preserving their own religious beliefs and ways of life. The influence of Islam gradually grew.

Facsimiles of Prescriptions Worth 1,000 in Gold and Supplement to Prescriptions Worth 1,000 in Gold

Sun Simiao (c. 581-682) was a famous physician in the period of the Sui and Tang dynasties. He wrote *Qian Jin Yao Fang* (*Prescriptions Worth 1,000 in Gold*) and *Qian Jin Yi Fang* (*Supplement to Prescriptions Worth 1,000 in Gold*). The books summed up the experiences and theories of his predecessors, collected large numbers of prescriptions and acupuncture data, and for the first time listed cases of illnesses among children and women, initiating the classification of diseases and providing an important reference for the study of traditional Chinese medicine.

Comments on Laws of the Tang Dynasty (*Tang Lù Shu Yì*) is a law book that interpreted *The Laws of the Yonghui Reign* (*Yonghui Lù*). Published in 653, it has 12 parts and 30 volumes. Its basic content included criminal law, civil law, procedural law and administrative law, as people categorize them today. The ancient states of Japan, Korea and Vietnam generally emulated this code. It is regarded as a representative work of the ancient Chinese legal system.

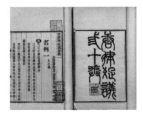

Facsimile of Comments on Laws of the Tang Dynasty

7th-11th centuries: Silver coins were introduced in Europe, which later became the pound, shilling and pence system of money.

Newly Revised Materia Medica

Newly Revised Materia Medica, alternatively called Tang Materia Medica, was the first national pharmacopoeia in Chinese history — published by the Tang government in 659. Of all the 53 volumes of the giant tome, the first volume is a table of contents, and the next 20 volumes are the Materia Medica, the main body with records of over 800 medicines, 114 of which were added anew. In this section, detailed information for each remedy was written down, including properties, tastes, smells, localities, collection, production, functions, and benefits. The 25 "illustrated" volumes depict the medicines, while the 7-volume "Explanatory Notes" provides captions for the illustrations. From its release until the mid-10th century, Newly Revised Materia Medica served as a main textbook for Chinese physicians.

Facsimile of Newly Revised Materia Medica

Yan Liben

Emperors of Past Dynasties (detail)

Yan Liben (?-673) was a Tang artist. Coming from a distinguished family of artists and calligraphers, he was skilled in painting figures and portraits. He painted with vigorous and forceful lines, in colors of ancient elegance and serenity, paying special attention to the portrayal of clothing, manners and facial expressions of figures, to convey different temperaments, individual characters and appearances. His paintings Sedan Chair and Emperors of Past Dynasties have been handed down to today.

Monk Huineng, founder of Southern Sect of Chan Buddhism

A new school of Buddhism — the Southern Sect of Chan (Zen) was set up in the early Tang Dynasty. Its founder was Monk Huineng (638-713), who was born in Guangdong. He believed that everyone was born with buddha nature and could attain Buddhahood in a way of sudden enlightenment. So he opposed practicing Buddhism through generations of tedious rites, and believed in seeking moksha (liberation) through peaceful secular living. Later, he made great efforts to advocate his theory of sudden enlightenment at Caoxi in Shaozhou, establishing consequently a direct branch of the Chan Sect. His Southern Sect brought Buddhism closer to the everyday life of common people, and also produced an evident impact on literature, arts, and the Confucian school of idealistic philosophy.

◎ 661-750: The Umayyad Dynasty of the Arab Empire.
◎ 668: Silla defeated Koguryo and unified the Korean Peninsula.

● Export of porcelain

● Wu Zetian (r. 690-705)

● Fazang, founder of the Garland School of Buddhism

● Techniques in making ceramics improved notably in the Tang Dynasty. Craftspeople could now make tri-colored glazed pottery (yellow, brown and green) at temperatures as high as 1,100°. Beginning in the Tang, Chinese porcelain began to be exported to Japan, Korea, India, Iran, Iraq, Egypt, and Europe. Porcelain ware was transported either by land or sea: by land, it was traded to Central and West Asia and Europe via the Silk Road; by sea, it went to Japan, the Korea Peninsula, South and West Asia, and North and East Africa. The sea route was known as the "Porcelain Route."

Portrait of Wu Zetian

● Wu Zetian (624-705) was the daughter of a timber trader. She became a palace maid at the age of 14. While in the imperial palace, she learned to engage in politics, and became empress of Li Zhi, Tang Emperor Gaozong (r.650-683), in 655, becoming involved in court affairs. After the death of Emperor Gaozong, she chose, one after another, two inept princes as puppet emperors in order to control power. In 690, she mounted the throne and changed the dynastic title to "Zhou." Under her 15-year rule, she continued to follow her husband's policies, but she appointed ruthless officials to suppress those who opposed her. In 705, Emperor Zhongzong Li Xian took the throne and restored the Tang Dynasty.

● Fazang (643-712) was a monk from the Western Regions. He participated in the translation of the 80-volume *Garland Sutra*. He made a thorough study of the sutra, and developed his theories about the interdependence of all things, the ten philosophical ideas, the four dharma realms, and unity of all phenomena as viewed from six characteristics. On this basis, he organized Buddhist theories and schools of various periods into a hierarchy, placing the Garland Sutra above all others, ultimately setting up the Garland School of Buddhism.

Tri-colored glazed pottery horse, Tang Dynasty

◎ 694: Manicheism introduced into China, known as *Mingjiao* or the "Teaching of the Light" in China.

◎ 697: The Venetian Republic was established, which developed into a plutocracy in the 10th century.

Liu Zhiji and Work of History

Zhang Xu and his "Wild Cursive Hand"

Wu Daozi

Liu Zhiji (661-721) was an official historian whose function was to supervise the compilation of national history. He wrote 49 articles for *Work of History* (*Shitong*), which explicated the theory, methods and skills of historiography, organizational systems of official historians, as well as the merits and demerits of history books, thus elevating Chinese historians from only recording history to new heights of analyzing and commenting historians, history books and historiography. For the first time in history, he proposed that historians must have the basic qualifications of historical knowledge, integrity and presentation skills. Historic integrity, or integrity to historical facts, was considered the most important of all.

Facsimile of *Work of History*

Four Poems (detail), by Zhang Xu

Chinese calligraphy is based on written characters, and constitutes a unique artistic form, with the composition of dot and line strokes as well as arrangement of space. The cursive hand is typically representative of this artistic form, and the emergence of the "wild cursive hand" was the zenith of its development. Zhang Xu (675-785), a Tang calligrapher, had to drink wine before he began working. When he became inebriated, he would pace wildly, and then take up his brush to begin writing, with the brush moving and the ink flying, until the work was done without interruption. Hence the name, "wild cursive hand."

Wu Daozi (?-760) was a Tang court artist. He was particularly skilled in painting religious murals and Buddhist and Daoist figures, but was also gifted at landscapes. He was known as the "sage painter" in the history of Chinese painting. On the basis of emulating the painting techniques of his predecessors, he formed his own style — profuse and jumbled strokes, magnificence of composition, yet with simple and light colors. He often used the shapes of orchid leaves or water shield to depict pleats and ribbons on dresses as if they were flying in the breeze, thus winning fame as "Wu's Ribbons in the Wind."

Eighty-seven Celestials (detail), by Wu Daozi

710-784: Japan moved its capital to Nara, the first permanent capital in Japanese history. This came to be known as the "Nara period."

● Li Longji,
Tang Emperor Xuanzong (r. 712-756)

● Great Prosperity of the
Kaiyuan Years (713-741)

Portrait of Li Longji

● When Li Xian, Tang Emperor Zhongzong died in 707, Li Longji (685-762), Empress Wu Zetian's grandson, rose among a good number of successors, ascending the throne in 712. He was known as Emperor Xuanzong, who reigned the longest during the Tang. Xuanzong did his best to make the country prosperous by straightening up the administrative system, rectifying previous harmful policies and stabilizing the chaotic political situation, opening up what came to be known as the "Great Prosperity of the Kaiyuan Years." In his late reign, however, he placed undue trust in his eunuchs, gave key positions to treacherous court officials, and indulged in sensual pleasures, making it more and more difficult to control regional secessionist forces. He finally gave up his throne in tears, during the armed rebellion led by An Lushan and Shi Siming, leaving the ruins of the country to his successor.

● "Kaiyuan" was the reign title of Emperor Xuanzong from 713 to 741. During this period, he rectified the harmful policies of his predecessor and established a clean and uncorrupt government. He also reduced taxes on the people, and built water conservancy projects. As a result, production developed, the treasury grew, and the population increased fourfold. The Silk Road was cleared, increasing the volume of traders from Persia and the Arab Empire, with foreign trade growing tremendously. Sea transport also saw development. Envoys from Japan, Korea and Southeast Asia swarmed into Chang'an. The thriving Tang Dynasty became the economic and cultural center of Asia.

Bohai (Balhae) Kingdom

Monk Yixing and the Dayan Calendar

Li Bai

▶ In the early Tang Dynasty, the Mohe people lived near the Songhua River, the lower Heilongjiang (Amur River) and the upper Tumen River. The Mohe were divided into various groups, the most powerful being the Black Water Mohe and the Sumo Mohe. The Tang government took control over this region, and appointed a chief as governor. In 713, Da Zuorong (Dae Jo Young, 698-719), the Sumo chieftain, was granted the title of "Prefecture King of Bohai" by Tang Emperor Xuanzong. With the establishment of the state, the Bohai king adopted the political and economic structures of Tang China, as well as Chinese written characters. He also sent regular envoys to pay tribute to the Tang, as well as dispatched students to study in the Imperial College.

Balhae green-glazed animal head

▶ Monk Yixing (673-727), original name Zhang Sui, was accomplished in the calendric system and astronomy. He co-invented an astronomical instrument called the water-powered armillary sphere. In 724, he organized a large-scale astronomical survey using this invention and successfully measured the length of the meridian. After this survey, he created the new Dayan Calendar according to his observations. He deduced a fairly accurate law on the speed changes of the sun's ecliptic movement.

Portrait of Li Bai

▶ There were many poets in the Tang Dynasty, yet Li Bai (701-762) enjoyed the greatest reputation for his unsurpassed achievements. His political disappointment, audacious temperament, and the prosperous and highly developed situation of the Tang Dynasty all inspired him to become the poet who could compose "100 poems after drinking to his heart's content." Nearly 1,000 of his poems have been handed down. They have a strong, uplifting artistic appeal, the language lucid and smooth, the meter harmonious and varied, and the imagination rich and uninhibited. Li Bai is an outstanding representative of the romantic poetry of ancient China.

© 726-843: The Age of Iconoclasm in the Byzantine Empire.

King of Yunnan

Wang Wei

Yang Guifei

In the early Tang Dynasty, six tribes settled around Erhai Lake in southwest China, known as the "Six Zhaos." During the Kaiyuan era (713-741, Emperor Xuanzong), with the support of Tang China, Piluoge, chieftain of the Nanzhao (South Zhao) people, successively united the Six Zhaos, and established the Nanzhao kingdom. In 738, Piluoge was granted the title of "King of Yunnan" by Emperor Xuanzong, with the Nanzhao kingdom maintaining close links with Tang China. In the following years, despite internecine conflicts, economic and cultural exchanges between the two never ceased, and the Nanzhao region made unprecedented advances.

Wang Wei (701-761) came from an official's family. As he experienced great frustrations in his official career, he later lived in seclusion and read Buddhist scriptures. A poet and artist, in his early life he wrote frontier poems full of passion and uninhibited feelings, but later mainly painted pastoral landscapes to convey his interests and tastes as a hermit and Buddhist. With subtle color applied, his paintings conveyed deep conception with unique artistic charm and appeal. Therefore, Wang Wei gained fame for his style of "painting in poetry" and "poetry in painting."

Snow on the Yangtze River (detail), by Wang Wei

Yang Yuhuan (719-756), often referred to as Yang Guifei (Guifei then the highest rank for imperial consorts), was born to a local official's family in Shanxi. She was promoted as the highest-ranking concubine in 745. The emperor's deep love for her brought her whole family fame and wealth; and her cousin Yang Guozhong was even made prime minister. Influenced by her, Emperor Xuanzong indulged himself in women and diversions, leading to the state's corruption and instability. After the "An-Shi Rebellion" broke out, Emperor Xuanzong fled to Sichuan with Yang Guifei. On their way to Sichuan, his soldiers rebelled, executed Yang Guozhong and strangled Yang Guifei. Emperor Xuanzong then resigned from the throne to live in melancholy.

Early 8th century: *Beowulf*, the earliest and most complete heroic epic in Britain, was composed.

Polo's popularization

Tang Dynasty tales

Monk Jianzhen's eastern journey to Japan

Polo, called "jiju" in the Tang Dynasty, was a sport combining skill and entertainment. The players, on horseback, were equipped with long-handled mallets for hitting a soft ball. This sport was very popular during the Tang. Some key enthusiasts were Chinese emperors. Emperor Xuanzong raised many racehorses in the imperial family, and ordered military forces to also practice polo. Polo then was also an entertainment for women in the imperial palace, with specially trained women's polo teams.

The Tang Dynasty was the golden age for poetry, as well as for tales. The Tang tale was a new literary form developed from the traditional short anecdote. It incorporates historical memoir, poetry, prose and folksongs. Its themes range from love, history and politics, to heroism and deities. Among them, the romantic tales were the most famous, such as *The Story of Yingying*, *Visiting the Immortals' Cave*, *Tales of Three Dreams* and *The Curly Bearded Man*. This literary form also experienced some changes, with its focus shifting from plot to characters.

Statue of Monk Jianzhen in Toshodaiji Temple

Monk Jianzhen (687-763), born in Yangzhou, taught the Buddhist canon in Daming Temple. In 753, Jianzhen landed in Kyushu, and began 10 years of preaching in Japan. He first introduced Buddhist ordination in Todaiji Temple in Nara, and established the Ritsu school of Japanese Buddhism. In 759, he set up the Toshodaiji Temple in Nara, in the style of the Tang temples and ordained the Japanese emperor and officials. In 763, he died in Japan. His disciples made a dry-lacquer statue of him, still found in Toshodaiji Temple.

Playing Polo

Facsimile of *The Story of Yingying*

© 750-1258: The Abbasid Dynasty of the Arab Empire.

An Lushan Rebellion (755-763)

Du Fu

In the early 8th century, Tang Emperor Xuanzong set up the post of military governor in China's border areas to prevent foreign invasion. Military governors were granted with military and financial power, giving them an opportunity to develop their own forces, separate from the central government. An Lushan (703-757), originally a low-ranking official, was later promoted as military governor of Pinglu, Fanyang and Hedong, because he was very clever and had gained the emperor's trust. In 755, An Lushan rebelled against the Tang Dynasty. He sacked Luoyang and enthroned himself as the "Emperor of Dayan." He then occupied and looted Chang'an (today's Xi'an). Emperor Xuanzong fled to Sichuan. His son Li Heng regained Chang'an with the military assistance from the Huihe, the ancestry group of the Uygur ethnic group, and finally suppressed the An Lushan rebellion in 763. However, this did not halt the decline of the Tang Dynasty.

Portrait of Du Fu

Du Fu enjoyed the same reputation as Li Bai, and was famed as the "sage poet." Compared with Li Bai's romantic style, Du Fu's poems were realist, truthfully recording the social and political life of the Tang Dynasty, from prosperity to decline, and expressing his deep sympathy for the people's sufferings. Many of his poems came to be known as "history through poetry." His poems reflect different poetic styles, their meter and rhyme scheme precise and exact, the antithesis formed by lines matching in sound as well as in sense, and the language concise. His poems became the model for *lüshi*, a classical form of eight lines. More than 1,400 of his poems have been handed down.

Emperor Xuanzong's Journey to Sichuan, depicting the emperor's flight during a rebellion

752-911: The Carolingian Dynasty of the Frankish Kingdom.

● Lu Yu and *Classic of Tea*

● There is a saying in Chinese history: "Drinking tea arose during the Tang and became popular in the Song Dynasty." Drinking tea became very popular among the Tang nobility and refined men of letters. Teahouses at fairs were crowded with tea drinkers. Poems themed in tea emerged one after another. People during the Tang Dynasty invented a tea processing method called "steaming the green." In 780, Lu Yu wrote *Classic of Tea*, after studying the tea-drinking habits and customs of different regions and summarizing tea-making experiences. The book described the entire process of brewing tea and knowledge of picking tea-leaves, processing tea, tea sets and tea drinking etiquette, thus laying the foundation for China's tea ceremony. In this period, China's tea culture took shape, and was introduced to Japan and other countries.

Facsimile of
Classic of Tea

Tea-Horse Trade

The tea-horse trade was a policy and trade system of ancient times, under which the government exchanged tea for horses in the regions inhabited by ethnic minorities in Qinghai, Gansu, Sichuan, Yunnan and Tibet. It was initiated in the Tang, continued in the Song Dynasty, and grew most prosperous during the Ming. It gradually declined, beginning in the Qianlong reign of the Qing Dynasty. Through almost 1,000 years, all dynasties set up a special administrative unit in charge of the trade, such as the "Tea and Horse Department" of the Ming, opening a thriving trade route, the "Ancient Tea-Horse Road." In fact, the commodities transported and traded along this route included not only tea and horses. Silk, cotton cloth and ironware from the Central Plains, and furs, leather, gold and traditional medicines (such as caterpillar fungus and fritillary bulbs) from northwest China, also became important commodities for the trade.

● *Fanzhen*, local military regimes of the Tang (763-960)

● *Fanzhen*, literally "vassal's town," was originally a prefectural-level military command set up in the early Tang Dynasty to administer local military forces. Later, the power of the local military commands was extended to civilian affairs and transcended that of the prefecture governors. By the 9th century, there were more than 40 "vassals' towns" that controlled the majority of the northern territory of the Tang Dynasty. They ignored or evenchallenged the central government's rulings. The imperial court tried many times to reduce their power, but failed every time. The ongoing conflicts between the central government and these *de facto* local military regimes depleted the imperial treasury and contributed to the downfall of the Tang Dynasty. The chaotic situation did not end until the Northern Song Dynasty reunited China in the mid-10th century.

Yang Yan and his tax reform

Nanchan Temple

Papermaking technology introduced to Arab world

▶ The Nanchan Temple, located in Lijia Village, southwest of the seat of Wutai County in Shanxi Province, was reconstructed in 782 (unclear when originally built). It is China's oldest existing Tang temple. With its single-layer eaves, gable roof and brackets on top of its pillars to support the eaves, the temple has a very simple beam structure and has no pillars inside the hall. All these elements reflect a typical Tang style. This temple is a testament to the high architectural level of the Tang Dynasty.

▶ In 751, the Tang Dynasty battled the Dashi (ancient name for Arab countries) in Dallus (now Zhambyl, in Kazakhstan), then an important city in Central Asia. Some Tang soldiers held captive by the Arab troops began to teach papermaking technology and helped establish a paper factory in Samarqand. In 794, under the guidance of Chinese workers, the Arab Empire built a new paper factory in Baghdad. From then on, they began to use paper to record government documents and archives. Later, China's papermaking technology was introduced to Syria, Egypt, Morocco, Spain, Italy and other foreign countries.

▶ Yang Yan (727-781), style name Gongnan, was prime minister during Tang Emperor Dezong's (r. 779-805) reign. On witnessing the draining of the Tang treasury, he started to reform the tax systems in 780. He abolished China's former poll tax structure. A property tax was levied based on the size of each family's landholdings and wealth. Since taxes were collected twice a year, in the summer and autumn, the new tax system became known as Liangshui Fa (Two Taxes Law). Although the reform did not much help the Tang Dynasty's financial situation, it marked a breakthrough in China's taxation history.

Nanchan Temple

◯ 8th-17th centuries: The Mali Empire in West Africa.

► Bai Juyi

Portrait of Bai Juyi

► Bai Juyi (772-846), style name Letian, was an official when young, but not very successful in his career. However, his poetry became very famous, emphasizing simplicity and reality. He called for a poetry that was socially responsible and reflected the current sufferings of the people. His representative works include the long narrative poems, *Chang Hen Ge* [*Song of Eternal Sorrow*] and *Pipa Xing* [*Song of the Pipa Player*], and the satirical poems of *Qin Zhong Xing* [*Traveling in the Land of Qin*] and *Xin Yuefu* [*New Yuefu*]. In his later years, Bai believed in Buddhism, often composing poems while drinking. His poems composed during this period were serene or even gloomy.

► Classical Prose Movement

► The Classical Prose Movement was a literary movement initiated by Han Yu (768-824), to reform the Tang writing style and literary language. He advocated the principle that writing must express one's thoughts and reflect the society. Thus he incorporated classical prose into a new concise and clear style of writing, to replace the florid *pianwen* or parallel prose style, which had been popular since the Wei, Jin and Southern and Northern Dynasties. His movement was greatly supported by another famous literary figure, Liu Zongyuan. The Classical Prose Movement had a great influence on the literary arena of the next millennium from the Tang Dynasty onwards.

Portrait of Han Yu

Han Yu and Liu Zongyuan

Han Yu (768-824) and Liu Zongyuan (773-819) were both great literary masters of the Tang Dynasty. Their prose writings represent an important literary achievement of the Tang. Han Yu's essays were strong in argument, while his poems emphasized novelty. Liu Zongyuan's travelogues were reflective, deftly interweaving his thoughts and reasoning into descriptions of scenery. They were both strong proponents of the prose style of the pre-Qin Dynasty, rather than the *pianwen* (parallel prose) of the Han, Wei and the Six Dynasties. They stressed that essays should convey social responsibility and should avoid platitudes. Han and Liu's great influence on the literary style of the Tang and later dynasties gave them the joint name of "Han-Liu." Han Yu, in particular, was referred to as "the greatest proseman" by people of later generations.

Liu Zongyuan

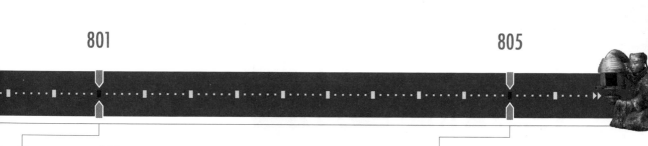

▶ **Du You and his** *Tongdian*   ▶ **Liu Yuxi**   ▶ **Yongzhen Reformation**

▶ Du You (735-812) was a politician, historian and prime minister of the Tang Dynasty. He finished his masterpiece, *Tongdian* (*Comprehensive Institutions*) in 801. This book comprises 200 volumes in total, covering 9 sectors, including economic, electoral, military and legal systems of China, government institutions, and local governmental organizations. It records the development of various institutions and systems from ancient times to the 8th century. It is the first encyclopedia of Chinese institutions and initiated a new style of classification for books on the history of institutions.

Facsimile of
Comprehensive Institutions

▶ Liu Yuxi (772-842), a famous Tang poet, styled Mengde, was born to a scholar's family. He

Liu Yuxi

created a great number of folk poems, which reflected people's lives and customs of that time. His poetry was natural, refreshing, healthy, and full of vigor and fun. His satirical poems often used imageries to satirize social phenomena and government officials. Good examples are *Zhuzhi Ci* (*Bamboo Branch Song*) and *Chatian Ge* (*Song of Planting Seedlings*).

▶ From the mid Tang Dynasty, the court gradually fell into the hands of corrupt eunuchs, sounding a warning to the emperor and bureaucrats. In 805, the first year of the Yongzhen era, Emperor Shunzong appointed Wang Shuwen (753-806) as a Hanlin official to recover financial and military command from the eunuchs. Their interests threatened, the eunuchs and corrupt officials staged a coup, placed the emperor under house arrest, and killed upright officials who supported the reformation. Later that year, Emperor Shunzong was forced to abdicate, and died of illness the next year. The 146-day restoration is known in Chinese history as "Yongzhen Reformation."

◎ 802-1431: The Khmer Empire period.

Strife between the Niu and Li factions (808-847)

The late Tang Dynasty was challenged by regional secessionism and internal conflicts in the central government. The most well-known conflict was the strife between the Niu and Li factions. The leader of the Niu faction was Niu Sengru (779-847), while the Li was led by Li Deyu (787-850). Niu and his partisans mostly had been selected through the imperial examinations, and thus advocated the imperial examination system; while Li and his partisans represented aristocrats and emphasized that high-ranking officials should be selected from dynastic official families. Regarding the problem of regional secessionism, the Niu insisted on negotiation while the Li supported suppression. The two factions fought with each other for more than 40 years, accelerating the Tang Dynasty's decline.

Li Jifu and *Gazetteer on the Prefectures and Counties of the Yuanhe Reign*

Facsimiles of *Gazetteer on the Prefectures and Counties of the Yuanhe Reign*

Li Jifu (758-814), style name Hongxian, was once the prime minister of the Tang Dynasty. He wrote the book *Yuanhe Junxian Zhi* (*Gazetteer on the Prefectures and Counties of the Yuanhe Reign*), based on extensive materials and documents he had collected. The book introduced each administrative region of the Tang Dynasty in terms of politics, economy and geography. As an encyclopedia of the Tang geography, it details the development, residences, mountains and rivers, streets and neighborhoods, local products, taxation, cultural relics, and other aspects of all administrative regions.

Yan Zhenqing and Liu Gongquan

Yan Zhenqing (708-784), a Tang calligrapher, after thoroughly studied previous calligraphy, incorporated the four calligraphy styles of *zhuan* (seal character), *li* (official script), *xing* (running hand) and *kai* (regular script) into the new "Yan" calligraphy style. The "Yan" style emphasized gracefulness, grandness, boldness and strength, and influenced the style of Tang calligraphy, also taking Chinese calligraphy to new realms. The other calligrapher, Liu Gongquan (778-865), influenced by Yan, created his own style, known as "Liu." The "Liu" style stressed firmness, grace, strength, compactness and fine structure. He is often referred to in combination with his famed predecessor, as "Yan-Liu."

The Yan style   The Liu style

Ganlu Coup d'etat

In 835, Emperor Wenzong of the Tang Dynasty attempted to get rid of domineering eunuchs, so as to regain power. This resulted in a plot hatched by Prime Minister Li Xun to ambush and kill Qiu Shiliang (781-843) and other eunuchs, after inviting them to a *ganlu* (dew) gathering one day. The plot was ultimately discovered and Wenzong was held hostage, and placed under house arrest until his eventual death, while Li Xun and his conspirators were executed. More than 1,000 people died in this coup d' etat, which became the most tragic imperial court incident in Chinese history.

Pottery eunuch figurine, Tang Dynasty

Abolition of Buddhism by Tang Emperor Wuzong

In the late Tang Dynasty, Buddhist monasteries were exempt from taxes, and monks from compulsory labor. Since Buddhism had flourished into a major religion in China, without these taxes the government suffered financially. In 845, the zealous Daoist Emperor Wuzong (r. 840-846) ordered the tabulation and verification of Buddhist monasteries and monks across the country, with all Buddhist temples to be demolished within a specified time, all gold and silver Buddha sculptures to be turned in to the national treasury, iron sculptures melted to produce farm tools, and bronze sculptures along with bells and chimes melted down to mint coins. Under imperial edict, over 4,600 Buddhist monasteries were pulled down, some 260,000 monks and nuns were compelled to return to their homes, more than 500,000 monastery servants were freed from labor, and monastery property and lands were confiscated. Buddhism was not the only religion affected. Emperor Wuzong also ordered the expulsion of Nestorian Christian and Zoroastrian clergy.

Woodblock printing of *Diamond Sutra*

Woodblock printing was one of the great inventions of ancient China. The process of woodblock making and printing: first, write characters on thin and semi-transparent soft paper; put the paper on a board with the written characters face down; and then carve the characters in the board through the paper, following the strokes of the characters, thus the characters on the board are reversed. The next step is to brush ink on the carved board and press a piece of paper onto it; finally, rub the paper evenly with a brush and peel it off — thus the characters are printed right onto the paper. In the late Tang Dynasty, woodblock printing reached its peak. The earliest woodblock publication marked with the year is the incomplete *Jin Gang Jing* (*Diamond Sutra*), published in 868 and now found in the Museum of London.

843: Conflict over the throne in the Charlemagne Empire ended; the Treaty of Verdun was signed, dividing the territory of the empire into three kingdoms.

● Huang Chao Rebellion (875-884)

● At the end of the Tang Dynasty, heavy taxes forced many peasants to leave their homes and become refugees. In 875, Huang Chao (?-884), an illicit salt dealer, led a rebellion. His forces swept over more than half of China, including the Central Plains (mid and lower reaches of the Yellow River), Jiangnan (south of Yangtze lower reaches), south of the Five Ridges (Guangdong and Guangxi), and Hubei and Hunan provinces. In 880, Huang Chao's forces sacked Chang'an (today's Xi'an) and Luoyang. He then enthroned himself and called his regime "Daqi." However, due to the lack of a stable base, his army was ultimately defeated by Tang general Li Keyong in 884. To the declining Tang Dynasty, this rebellion added fuel to the fire.

● Mogao Grottoes of Dunhuang

Buddhist sculptures at Mogao Grottoes

Apsaras fresco at Mogao Grottoes

● The Mogao Grottoes, located at the eastern foot of Mingsha Mountain, 25 km southeast of Dunhuang, Gansu Province, are on five levels and stretch over 1,200 m in a south-north direction. There are 492 caves with 45,000 sq m of frescos and over 2,100 color sculptures. Started in the 4th century, the Mogao Grottoes took about a millennium to complete. The Tang Dynasty was the peak of grotto art. The frescos and sculptures are mostly themed with Buddhist tales and figures. They serve as a testament to the development of Buddhist sculptural arts from the 6th to 14th centuries.

◎ 882: Igor, Rurik's son, conquered Kiev and established Kiev Rus (?-1240), the preliminary form of Russia.

907 - 960

The Five Dynasties ● **Ten Kingdoms**

Portrait of Zhu Wen

● In the last few years of the Tang Dynasty, the central government was very weak. But none of the regional powers had their own states, until Zhu Wen established the Later Liang Dynasty in 907. Zhu Wen (852-912) originally served under the rebel Huang Chao. When the Huang Chao Rebellion was about to fail, he surrendered to the Tang Dynasty and helped to put down the rebellion forces. He gradually amassed military power over most of northern Chinese territory and deposed the Tang. Zhu took the throne and established his Liang Dynasty (history termed "Later Liang"), but this regime was unstable. After 16 years it was replaced by the Later Tang, which only 13 years later was overthrown by the Later Jin. After that, two more brief dynasties emerged, the Later Han and the Later Zhou. Over a mere half century, the country experienced five dynasties. This period in Chinese history is referred to as the "Five Dynasties."

The Five Dynasties and Ten Kingdoms		
Dynasty/Kingdom	**Capital**	**Period**
Later Liang	Bian (Kaifeng, Henan)	907-923
Later Tang	Luoyang	923-936
Later Jin	Bian (Kaifeng, Henan)	936-947
Later Han	Bian (Kaifeng, Henan)	947-950
Later Zhou	Bian (Kaifeng, Henan)	951-960
Wu	Yangzhou	892-937
Former Shu	Chengdu	891-925
Wuyue	Hangzhou	893-978
Min	Changle (Fuzhou, Fujian)	893-945
Southern Han	Guangzhou	904-971
Nanping (Jingnan)	Jingzhou (Jiangling, Hubei)	907-963
Chu	Changsha	896-951
Later Shu	Chengdu	925-965
Southern Tang	Jinling (Nanjing, Jiangsu)	937-975
Northern Han	Taiyuan	951-979

● While northern China suffered the frequent changeover of the Five Dynasties, in southern China and Shanxi emerged ten comparatively stable small kingdoms: the Wu and Southern Tang occupying the Yangtze River's middle and lower reaches, the Wuyue in Zhejiang, the Chu in Hunan, the Min in Fujian, the Southern Han in Guangdong and Guangxi, the Former Shu and Later Shu in Sichuan and Gansu, the Jingnan in Jiangling, and the Northern Han in central Shanxi. During this period southern China was relatively stable, thus the Yangtze delta area became more economically developed, and South China Sea's foreign trade more prosperous.

▶ *Jiaozi* – the World's earliest banknote

▶ In the early 10th century, wealthy Sichuan merchants together issued a type of paper money — *jiaozi*, later widely used in commercial trade. *Jiaozi*, made of standard paper, was painted with designs of houses and people. With a signature and secret marks on it, *jiaozi* was difficult to counterfeit, thus qualifying as paper currency. In 1003, the right of issuing *jiaozi* was taken over by the government. It became a legal currency used by the entire country.

A *Jiaozi* sample

▶ Introduction of Chiem rice

Portrait of Wang
Shenzhi, King of Min

▶ A prominent feature of China's agriculture is that northern China grows wheat while the south grows rice. Chinese people started to cultivate rice as their staple food in early history. In 910, Wang Shenzhi (862-925), king of Min, introduced Chiem rice into Fujian from central southern Vietnam. It was gradually popularized in south China. Chiem rice, a variety of early Indica rice, was very adaptable, with a short maturation period and high yield; thus it was able to feed more people, contributing to increases in China's population.

▶ Later Zhou Emperor Shizong laid the foundation for unification

▶ Emperor Shizong (r. 954-959) of the Later Zhou rose to power in the turbulent era of the Five Dynasties and Ten Kingdoms. The national strength of the Later Zhou was substantially improved through political and military reforms and economic development. The emperor also undertook a series of military expeditions to conquer the Later Shu and Southern Tang. He further ventured north to attack the Khitan people, laying a firm foundation for the unification of China by the Song Dynasty.

© Early 10th century: Constantinople became the biggest city in Europe.
© 918: Koryo (today's Korea) established.

916 - 1125

● When the Tang Dynasty was on the verge of falling as local military forces tried to break away from the central government, an aggressive northern tribe — the Khitan rose. Led by the Yelü clan, they established the Khitan Empire in 916 and officially adopted the name "Liao" in 947. The Liao Dynasty witnessed nine emperors, and lasted more than two centuries. During this period, there were still two other empires, the Northern Song and Western Xia. The Liao Dynasty's territory expanded from the Mongolian grasslands to the North China Plain, from Koryo in the east to Altai Mountain in the west. It blocked the Central Plains area from direct contact with Central and West Asia.

Khitan Man Wearing Traditional Hairstyle

Silver bridles with gold gilding

● Born into an aristocratic Khitan family, Yelü Abaoji (872-926) in his 30s took command of Khitan political and military power. In 907, he was elected Khan. In 916, Abaoji abolished the traditional ruling structure, and established the Khitan Empire in its place. In court, Abaoji adopted Chinese court formalities and set up new administrative institutions. He also borrowed largely from Chinese culture, ordering the development of a Khitan script, and building the capital along the lines of Chang'an. To expand territory and augment national power, the ambitious ruler also undertook large-scale military expeditions, but died of illness during one such expedition in 926. As the founder of the Liao Dynasty, Abaoji contributed greatly to the unification of the northern nomadic peoples, whose political, economic and cultural development improved considerably under his reign.

◎ 919 -1024: The Saxon Dynasty of Germany.
◎ 927: The seven kingdoms period in Britain ended and the Kingdom of England was established.
◎ 935-936: Koryo captured Silla and Baekje, and united Korea Peninsula.

960 - 1126

● **Northern Song Dynasty**   ● Zhao Kuangyin established the Song Dynasty

Zhao Kuangyin

● In 960, Zhao Kuangyin, a general of the Later Zhou, established the Song Dynasty, which saw the reunification of China's territory. With a history of 300 years and 18 emperors, the dynasty spanned two periods: the Northern Song from 960 to 1126, basing its capital in Kaifeng; and the Southern Song after Kaifeng was occupied by the Jin forces, with the capital moved in 1127 to Lin'an (in present-day Hangzhou). The Song Dynasty saw great growth in the economy, arable land and agricultural production, as well as technological innovations in porcelain, textiles, papermaking, shipbuilding and mining. Booming trade brought progress in the financial industry. Paper currency started to circulate, and foreign trade also flourished. Confucianism experienced resurgence in the form of Neo-Confucianism. New literary forms represented by *ci* poetry pushed Chinese culture to new heights. Even as the Song was enjoying its cultural prosperity, it was greatly threatened by the Jin Dynasty founded by the Jurchens. In 1126, the Northern Song Dynasty was ended after its capital Kaifeng was seized by the Jin army.

The busy streets of Bianliang, capital of the Northern Song Dynasty

● Zhao Kuangyin (927-976) joined the army in the Later Han Dynasty, and controlled the Later Zhou Dynasty's military forces. In 960, he deceived the central government, fabricating Khitan forces' attack of the border, thus leading his troops to the north to "fight." When he arrived at Chenqiao in the outskirts of Kaifeng, he launched a coup d'etat and enthroned himself. He established the Song Dynasty and set up its capital in Kaifeng. He was credited for reuniting China after prolonged fragmentation and chaos.

© 945-968: The "Rebellion of Twelve Military Chiefs" in Vietnam.

Military power relieved over cups of wine

Fan Kuan and his *Travelers amid Mountains and Streams*

Li Yu

In order to eradicate local secessionist forces that had arisen in the Tang Dynasty, and halt their threat to the central government, Zhao Kuangyin in the second year of his reign (961) invited Shi Shouxin (928-984) and other generals and regional officers who controlled military power to several banquets. He persuaded them to give up their military power, and instead accumulate more wealth to prepare for more comfortable lives. In this way, the central government quickly shrunk regional military, civil and financial powers, and improved administrative efficiency. Zhao's move greatly contributed to the Song Dynasty's golden age in economy, culture, science and technology.

Travelers amid Mountains and Streams

Fan Kuan (birth and death dates unknown), a landscape painter during the early Northern Song Dynasty, lived as a recluse in the mountains. His only surviving work is *Travelers amid Mountains and Streams*, painted on silk, 206 cm tall and 103 cm wide. In the painting, the cliffs appear as if cut out by axes. The mule train on the path in the foreground, dwarfed by the magnificent mountains, expresses the artist's resolve to conquer the mountains.

Li Yu (937-978) was the last Southern Tang emperor in the Five Dynasties and Ten Kingdoms era. Lacking the political ability to govern, Li devoted most of his time to poetry. His early poems centered on court life and love affairs, while his later works expressed grief over his lost empire, after it had been overthrown by the Song Dynasty. A captive of the Song, Li described his longing for his country and nostalgia for the old days, in his masterpieces *Yu the Beauty*, *Washing Sand in the Stream*, and *The Raven's Evening Cry*.

Portrait of Li Yu

◎ 962-1806: The Holy Roman Empire of the German nation.
◎ 980: Vietnam's Lê Hoàn established the Tien Le Dynasty.

▶ Woodblock printing of the *Tripitaka* (971-983)

▶ Chanyuan Alliance ▶ Jingdezhen Porcelain

▶ The Song Dynasty paid great attention to collecting, preserving, editing, compiling and utilizing books. It invested extensive capital in printing encyclopedias and Buddhist scriptures. The woodblock *Tripitaka* published in the early Song Dynasty is a fine example. This version has three categories, *Vinaya Pitaka* (code of ethics), *Sutra Pitaka* (accounts of the Buddha's teachings) and *Abhidharma Pitaka* (canons), and included Buddhist works from India, China and other countries. Totaling more than 5,000 volumes and 76 million Chinese characters on over 79,000 two-sided woodblocks, the engraving and printing of this collection took 12 years to finish. This version became the standard model for official and unofficial republications of the *Tripitaka*, which were given to Japan, Korea, Vietnam and other countries.

▶ In 1004, the Liao troops launched a large-scale attack on the Song Dynasty. They besieged Chanzhou on the north banks of the Yellow River. Advised by Prime Minister Kou Zhun (961-1023), Song Emperor Zhenzong himself led troops to Chanzhou. But not daring to fight the Liao troops, he insisted on a peace talk. The result was that the Song Dynasty agreed to pay annual tribute of 200,000 bolts of silk and 100,000 taels of silver to the Liao. The Liao troops retreated to Baigou River. As Chanzhou was also called Chanyuan, this treaty came to be referred to as the "Chanyuan Alliance."

▶ Jingdezhen (or Jingde Town), in northeast Jiangxi Province, began to produce porcelain from the 5th century onwards. During the Jingde reign (998-1003) of the Song Dynasty, the emperor assigned people to build official kilns to produce imperial ceramics. These ceramics were marked with the characters, "Made in the Jingde Reign," at the bottom — giving Jingdezhen its name. From then on, emperors of each dynasty sent supervisors to Jingdezhen to control the quality of imperial chinaware, producing millions of excellent pieces. Jingdezhen porcelain, originally white; later, it became even more diversified and refined, mainly blue and white or famille rose, with its enamelware the most famous.

○ 987-1328: The Capetian Dynasty of France.
○ 1010-1225: The Ly Dynasty of Vietnam.

1027

Private academies flourished

Library of the Yuelu Academy

Private academies appeared early in the 6th century, when they were found mostly in scenic mountains and areas. Renowned examples of that time include the Bailu Cave, Songyang, Yingtianfu and Yuelu academies. These private local schools taught Confucian classics to train political scholars for the country, or focused on theoretic research and teaching of different schools of thoughts, or simply provided a place for scholars and literati to gather together, enjoying food, composing poems and discussing classics and national affairs.

Wang Weiyi's acupuncture bronze statues

With the further development of Chinese acupuncture therapy, many new acupoints were discovered. In order to avoid confusion, Wang Weiyi, a medical officer of the Northern Song Dynasty, cast two hollowed-out life-size bronze human figures, each one marked with 559 acupoints. Since 107 of them had a second acupoint sharing the same name, the needle points on each bronze figure actually amounted to 666. The bronze figures were copied and used by the later dynasties as models for medical therapies and teaching and tests.

A bronze acupuncture statue

Ouyang Xiu and Song poetry and essay reforms

Portrait of Ouyang Xiu

Ouyang Xiu (1007-1072), who nicknamed himself "Zuiweng," or "Old Drunkard," was an acclaimed scholar, literary master and renowned literary leader of the early Northern Song Dynasty. He followed Han Yu's Classical Prose Movement, promoting the idea of reasoning through writing. He advocated a succinct, simple and natural style of writing. All his prose and political and narrative writings abided by that style. His style of writing greatly inspired the literature of later generations.

1038 - 1227

The Western Xia Kingdom ● Li Yuanhao (r. 1038-1048)

● The Western Xia was established by the Tangut people in northwest China. The Tangut people began their close contact with the Han at the end of the Tang Dynasty. In their intercourses, either aggressive or submissive, with the Song and Liao dynasties, they gradually developed into a local power. In 1038, Li Yuanhao proclaimed himself Emperor of Great Xia (known in Chinese history as Western Xia), and made Xingqing (now in Ningxia) his capital. In the following years, he adopted Song systems, gradually building a centralized kingdom, reforming the military system and creating the Western Xia's written language. The Western Xia, with the Tangut as the majority of the population and the Han, Turpan and Huihu as minorities, ruled northwest China for 190 years.

Western Xia imperial mausoleum

A fragment of a stele with Western Xia characters

Stone statue at the Western Xia imperial mausoleum

● Li Yuanhao (1003-1048) was the first emperor of the Western Xia. Dissatisfied with the Xia's subordination to the Song Dynasty, Li enacted a series of reforms upon accession to the throne. He ordered the discarding of Chinese surnames given by the Tang and Song dynasties, replacing them with Xia surnames. He changed clothing, ritual and music styles by following Xia traditions, and ordered the creation of a Xia script. The bureaucratic establishment was also subject to reforms that maintained Xia characteristics under the Song system. He also carried out military campaigns to expand territory. In 1038, Li proclaimed himself Emperor of the Western Xia, contending for power with the Song and Liao dynasties. A flexible foreign policy with the two powers was adopted, and this Tangut society saw considerable development in its politics, economy and society. A voracious and lustful tyrant, Li Yuanhao was murdered by his son in 1048.

1040

1041

● Gunpowder weapons

● Bi Sheng invented the movable-type printing system

● It was only from the Northern Song Dynasty that workshops began to produce gunpowder and gunpowder weapons. The book *Records of the Eastern Capital* [*Dongjing Ji*]

Sketch of an arrow with gunpowder

published in 1040 documents the production and uses of the main weapon using gunpowder at that time — the fireball. The many uses of fireballs were clearly defined, to produce smoke and poison gas, to burn, and to destroy. There were also other weapons using gunpowder, such as "pear-blossom" spears that were attached with gunpowder shafts and arrows with fire caltrops — packages filled with gunpowder and iron caltrops.

Sketch of a pear-blossom spear

● The movable-type printing system was invented by Bi Sheng, a woodblock carver of the Northern Song Dynasty. In the 1040s, Bi took sticky clay cubes and cut reversed characters in relief on them, then baked them in fire to harden them. These cubes became movable characters used for printing. To begin the printing process, he covered a framed iron plate with a mixture of pine resin, wax and paper ashes, and set the types close together on it; then he heated the plate to melt the paste. When the paste cooled and fastened the types, the plate was ready for printing. After printing was completed, he heated the plate again so that the types could be removed. The invention of movable types marked a new era in printing technology. Due to its cost-effectiveness and high-efficiency, it was quickly popularized throughout the world.

Printing mold using clay cubes

127

Shao Yong

Portrait of Shao Yong

Shao Yong (1011-1077), a philosopher of the Northern Song Dynasty, was knowledgeable and talented. Based on his knowledge of *I Ching* (*Book of Changes*) and Taoism, he created a cosmological chart that showed the direction of the Eight Trigrams and the array of the 64 hexagrams. He believed that the origin of the cosmos was "*Taiji*," literally meaning the "Supreme Ultimate," which was eternal, and that everything in the world changed according to the pattern as shown by his cosmologic chart. Shao represented the image-number approach in the Northern Song Dynasty.

Zhou Dunyi

Portrait of Zhou Dunyi

Zhou Dunyi (1017-1073), styled Maoshu, studied the classics when young, becoming a Neo-Confucianist philosopher. He thoroughly studied *I Ching*. On the basis of *I Ching* and Taoist philosophy, for the first time in Chinese history, he provided a detailed explanation of the origin and evolution of the cosmos. His *Diagram Explaining the Supreme Ultimate* (*Taiji Tu Shuo*), which incorporates nature, society and humans, holds that *Taiji* (the Supreme Ultimate) originates from *Wuji* (the Void). *Yang* is generated from *Taiji* in motion; while *yin* from *Taiji* in stillness. The combination of *yin* and *yang* generates everything. Zhou's philosophy marks the start of a synthesis of Confucianism, Taoism and Buddhism.

Zhang Zai and his benevolent philosophy

Zhang Zai (1020-1077), styled Zihou, was a philosopher of the Northern Song Dynasty. His most famous ethical doctrine was "all humans are my siblings and all living things are my companions." He argued that everyone had Heaven and Earth as their father and mother, and thus all were brothers and sisters; caring for others was like caring for one's own family. Though all living creatures were friends, they did not share absolute equality, instead being strictly classified.

Portrait of Zhang Zai

1043

● *Lixue* (the Study of Principle)

● Fan Zhongyan and Qingli Reform (1043-1044)

Portrait of
Fan Zhongyan

● From the 11th century, a group of Song Dynasty scholars, represented by Zhou Dunyi, Cheng Yi, Cheng Hao and Zhu Xi, reexamined pre-Qin Confucianism from cosmological and ontological perspectives and created, by incorporating Buddhist and Taoist ideas, a new theory — Neo-Confucianism, or *Lixue* (the Study of Principle). They believed that *li* (principle) is an objective, independent entity that gives rise to and controls everything in the universe. *Lixue* provides the basic ways of self-cultivation, the political ideas of how to rule a country, and the moral ethics for society. In the following eight centuries, Neo-Confucianism gradually dominated the intellectual and spiritual life of China and other East Asian countries, with a far-reaching influence on these cultures.

● Fan Zhongyan (989-1052), a politician of the Northern Song, was a righteous official who dared to speak up for the people. In the 3rd year of the Qingli reign of Emperor Renzong (1043), Fan submitted a 10-point proposal outlining his reform objectives to increase administrative efficiency, develop economy and strengthen national defense. However, his reforms met with opposition from groups of bureaucrats. Though a few reforms were put into effect, they were, together with the whole program, abolished within two years, and ultimately Fan was forced to leave the imperial court. Also a distinguished man of letters, Fan is remembered for his famous line in *Yueyang Tower*: "Be the first to bear worries, and be the last to enjoy comforts."

Yingxian Wooden Pagoda (1056-1195)

Yingxian Wooden Pagoda

The Sakya Pagoda, commonly know as the Yingxian Wooden Tower, is located in the Fogong Temple in northwest Yingxian County. Built in the Liao Dynasty, the octagonal pagoda stands 67.13 m tall, its first story being 30.27 m in diameter, and its brick base being 4.4 m in height. The nine-floor tower was built with 54 types of brackets, and over 60 types of beams, rafters and girders. The multi-tier design made the tower extremely firm in structure.

Cheng Yi and Cheng Hao

Cheng Yi (1033-1107) and Cheng Hao (1032-1085), philosophers of the Northern Song Dynasty, were both students of Zhou Dunyi. The brothers based their philosophies on the concept of *tianli* (heavenly principle). They argued that *li* dominates everything in the universe; the principle of heaven translates into destiny and the principle of man into human nature; relations between the ruler and the ruled and between father and sons are decided by the principle of heaven. The brothers had different views on how to comprehend *tianli*. Chen Yi thought of *tianli* as the origin of everything, and one should reach it through studying the *li* of everything. In contrast, Cheng Hao believed that one could comprehend *tianli* through self-cultivation.

Su Dongpo

Su Dongpo (1037-1101), also known as Su Shi, was a famous poet, painter, calligrapher, writer and politician of the Northern Song Dynasty. His poems were imaginative, uplifting and original; his essays expressive, liberal and rich in content; and his calligraphy works featured unrestrained, varied and rhythmic strokes. He liked to paint unusual rocks and trees and loved to collect curios. Su also cared about education; even when he was banished to remote Hainan Island, he tried his best to educate the people there.

Su Dongpo

© 1054: Christianity underwent a gradual schism that divided it into the Eastern Orthodox and Western Roman Catholic churches.

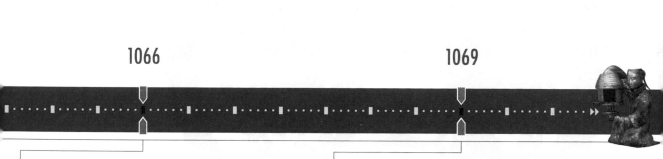

● Sima Guang and *Zizhi Tongjian* (1066-1084)

Portrait of Sima Guang

● In 1066, Sima Guang (1019-1086) was assigned the compilation of the book *Zizhi Tongjian* (*Comprehensive Mirror to Aid Governance*), which took 19 years to complete. The book includes official history as well as reliable sources of unofficial history, academic books, epigraphs and inscriptions. It chronologically narrates the history of China from the Warring States Period (475-221 BC) to the Five Dynasties Period (907-960), providing rulers with advice from previous dynasties to better rule the country. Sima Guang was upright, knowledgeable and intelligent, as well as highly accomplished in Chinese literature.

Manuscript of
Zizhi Tongjian

● Wang Anshi's reforms (1069-1076)

Portrait of Wang Anshi

● In 1069, Wang Anshi (1021-1086), chancellor of Song Emperor Shenzong, began his reforms in order to resolve the Song government's budget deficit and poverty among the peasantry. His reforms spanned political, military, economic, education, ethical and other aspects. His agricultural reforms, including massive construction of irrigation works, government loans to cultivators and taxes levied according to land area, were fully implemented and achieved positive results. Though Wang's reforms met huge resistance, they continued for nearly ten years, and finally achieved the progress intended.

© 1066: William (r. 1066-1087), Duke of Normandy, invaded England by crossing the ocean from France, and was acclaimed King of England.

Guo Xi and his *Early Spring*

Shen Kuo and his *Dream Pool Essays*

Guo Xi (1023-1085), a Northern Song royal court artist, initiated the theory of landscape painting known as "Three Perspectives." His famous work *Early Spring* depicted the changes of the earth when winter turns to spring. It vividly conveys the idea of spring even without colorful flowers or green trees. He applied his "three perspectives" to painting: "the high perspective" referring to the view from the riverside rocks in the foreground to distant peaks; "the deep perspective," the view from the front to rear mountains; and "the flat perspective," from close mountains to distant ranges. His techniques ingeniously aligned still and mobile objects into harmonious composition of his works.

Early Spring

Portrait of Shen Kuo

Shen Kuo (1031-1095), a Northern Song polymath scientist, wrote the book *Dream Pool Essays* [*Meng Xi Bitan*] around 1090. This is an annotative literary work that covers a wide range of topics, including mathematics, astronomy, calendric systems, geography, geology, climatology, physics, chemistry, weaponry, irrigation, architecture, history, literature, music, fine arts, animals, plants, and medicine. Of these, the section on science and technology takes up more than one third of the content. The book contains 26 volumes and 609 articles, many of which are faithful records of science and technology of that time, as well as the author's own achievements in scientific research. It is an excellent written record of contributions to natural science by ancient China, especially the Northern Song.

Facsimile of
Dream Pool Essays

○ 1073-1085: Roman Pope Gregory VII (1020-1085) used his power to initiate reform of the Catholic Church.
○ 11th century: Capitalism appeared in northern Italy.

Mi Fu

Mi Fu (1051-1107), a great Northern Song artist, was highly accomplished in calligraphy and painting. He was adept at reproducing ancient calligraphy styles. Mi first learned calligraphy from Liu Gongquan's style, renowned for well-structured, bold, sturdy strokes; then he followed Wang Xizhi's style, featuring uninhibited and vigorous brushwork. His surviving calligraphy works include: *Elegy to Empress Dowager Xiang* and *Calligraphy on Sichuan Silk*.

Calligraphy on Sichuan Silk (detail)

Compass first used for navigation

Replica of a floating magnetic needle compass

The Northern Song Dynasty witnessed the application of the magnetic needle compass for navigation, with the device also being greatly improved. The original compass was made of a magnetized needle piercing through a piece of rush and then placed in a bowl of water. The needle's two ends pointed south and north when the water was still. Later, an azimuth was carved on the edge of the water plate for more accurate navigation. From 1099 to 1102, Chinese seagoing vessels from the Guangzhou port began to use the floating magnetic needle compass.

"Chinatowns"

From the Tang Dynasty onwards, China's maritime trade with African and Central Asian countries flourished. Malays built a "trade empire" with Palembang as its center, on the island of Sumatra, so as to control trade on the Malay Peninsula and the Strait of Malacca. It functioned as a trade "intermediary" between China and overseas areas. During the several hundred years from the Tang to the Southern Song dynasties, many southern Chinese residents moved to Sumatra. Since the Tang Dynasty held great international prestige, those migrants called themselves the "Tang people," and thus the place where they were concentrated came to be called "Tang People's Street," or today's "Chinatowns."

○ 1096-1099: The First Crusade was launched, occupying Jerusalem.

Li Jie and his *Treatise on Architectural Methods*

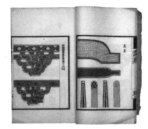

Facsimile of *Treatise on Architectural Methods*

Li Jie (?-1110), a Northern Song architect, took charge of many large-scale construction projects. He compiled the book *Treatise on Architectural Methods* (*Yingzao Fashi*), on the basis of his rich experience in architecture. This book contains 36 volumes, with 357 articles and 3,555 entries. As the most comprehensive architectural book in the world at that time, *Treatise on Architectural Methods* standardized building specifications, construction rules and regulations, as well as the monetary costs of labor and materials.

Zhang Zeduan's *Riverside Scene during Qingming Festival*

Zhang Zeduan, celebrated in the early 12th century, became an imperial court artist while touring and studying in the capital at the end of the Northern Song Dynasty. His famous painting *Riverside Scene during Qingming Festival* depicts the landscape of the Northern Song capital Kaifeng, along the banks of the Bianhe River during the Qingming (Pure Brightness) Festival. With total width of 528.7 cm and height of 24.8 cm, this horizontal scroll consists of three sections that capture scenes of the capital's outskirts in spring, the busy Bianhe River docks and bustling urban streets. There are more than 500 human figures with distinctive attire and expressions; streets and lanes; shops, official mansions, houses, huts and thatch-roofed houses; rivers, docks and ponds; boats and carriages; cows, sheep and camels; as well as old trees and green willows. This well-arranged hand scroll, invaluable as more than just a landscape painting, exemplifies a period of history.

Riverside Scene during Qingming Festival (detail)

1115 - 1234

● Jin Dynasty ● Wanyan Aguda (r. 1115-1123)

Jin Dynasty fresco, Preparing a Banquet

● The Jurchens (Nüzhen, a Tungus people) inhabited northeast China, including the Changbai Mountains and the drainage areas of the Songhua and Heilong rivers. In 1115, led by Wanyan Aguda, they established the Jin Dynasty and based their capital in Huining (now Acheng in Heilongjiang). In the decade that followed, the Jin Dynasty continued to expand its territory, moving its political center south to the Liao Dynasty's Nanjing (South Capital, now Beijing), renaming it Zhongdu ("Middle Capital"). In 1126, Jin forces launched a southern expedition to annihilate the Northern Song Dynasty. By then, Jin territory bordered Western Xia to the west and was separated from the Southern Song by the Qinling Mountains and the Huaihe River. In 1234, the Jin Dynasty, which lasted 120 years, collapsed due to attacks from both Mongols and the Southern Song.

● Wanyan Aguda (1068-1123) was a Jurchen Wanyan chieftain, as well as founder and first emperor of the Jin Dynasty. A talented leader with political and military ability, Aguda unified the Jurchen tribes at the beginning of the 12th century, and in 1115 established the Jin Dynasty at Huining (now Acheng, Heilongjiang Province). Over the following years, Aguda carried out a number of military campaigns against the Liao Dynasty, and saw final victory in 1123, shortly before his death. Establishing the Jurchen Empire and eliminating of the Liao, Aguda is remembered for his commitment to the unification and development of the Jurchen people. Apart from his military endeavors, Aguda also modernized the archaic system of organization, and ordered the creation of the Jurchen script modeled on regular Chinese script. Aguda, as an able emperor, played a decisive role in the development of Jurchen society.

Jurchen stele with
Jinshi scholars' names

Rebellions led by Fang La and Song Jiang (1119-1121)

In the late Northern Song Dynasty, two rebellions broke out, from people's resentment of growing corruption in the Song court. In 1119, Song Jiang (birth and death dates unknown) rallied a group of rebels in Mount Liang (now southern Dongping, Shandong), launching operations in Hebei and Shandong provinces. In 1121, defeated by the Song army in Haizhou (now Lianyungang, Jiangsu Province), the rebels surrendered to the court. *Outlaws of the Marsh*, a novel by Yuan Dynasty's Shi Naian, was inspired by the story of Song Jiang and his rebels. In 1120, Fang La (?-1121), a native of Qingxi, Muzhou (now Chun'an, Zhejiang Province), set up another rebel regime with some 10,000 rebels. This regime was crushed by a 150,000-strong Song army in 1121, and Fang was executed. Though eventually suppressed by gruesome means, the two rebellions delivered heavy blows to the reign of the Song Dynasty.

The Jingkang Incident

Song Emperor Qinzong

In 1126, Jurchen armies crossed the Yellow River and sacked Kaifeng, the Northern Song capital. After looting the most prosperous city in China of that time, they exiled Emperor Qinzong (r. 1125-1127), his father Emperor-in-retirement Huizong (r. 1100-1125), along with over 3,000 members of the imperial court to the freezing north. Some imperial members fled south of the Yangtze River. One of them, Zhao Gou, established the Southern Song Dynasty in Lin'an (now Hangzhou, Zhejiang). This mass banishment of the imperial family is known in Chinese history as the Jingkang Incident, since it occurred in the first year of the Jingkang reign of Emperor Qinzong. It marked the downfall of the Northern Song Dynasty.

1127 - 1279

Southern Song Dynasty
Yue Fei fought against the Jin troops (1127-1142)

In 1127, Zhao Gou (r. 1127-1162), the newly enthroned Song Emperor Gaozong, re-established his seat of government in Lin'an (now Hangzhou, Zhejiang). Known as the Southern Song Dynasty, the regime lasted for 152 years and nine emperors. As with its predecessor, the Southern Song court saw continuing political and military problems. Internal factional struggles prevailed in court politics, and a submissive stance towards peace became its foreign policy. In spite of its problems, Southern Song society coutinued with a period of stable development in economy, culture and technology. For its remarkable development in various respects, the Southern Song Dynasty became a new economic and cultural center in south China. In 1279, it was overthrown by the Mongol Yuan Dynasty from the north.

Yue Fei (1103-1142), born to a peasant family in Tangyin, Henan, joined the army and later became a general famed for his heroic resistance against the Jin (Jurchens) invasion. In 1140, Yue Fei and his troops, through great military skill, achieved a series of victories that drove the Jurchen invaders north of the Yellow River. There was a great possibility of recovering Kaifeng; however, Emperor Gaozong and his treacherous prime minister Qin Hui insisted on suing for peace, and ordered Yue Fei to withdraw his army. Yue Fei was called back to Lin'an and discharged from the military. Afterwards, he was framed and imprisoned. In 1142, he was executed by Qin Hui for a fabricated crime.

Southern Song stone inscription of paddy rice harvests

Yue Fei

● Li Qingzhao

● Treaty of Shaoxing

● Lu You

● Li Qingzhao (1084-1151), born to a wealthy family, lived an abundant life in her early years. She excelled in poetry, painting, calligraphy and epigraphy, and was best known for her *ci* poetry. Li's works feature subtlety, euphemism and melancholy elegance. They expressed the poet's sorrow over her personal misfortunes and that of her country.

Li Qingzhao

● After the "Jingkang Incident," the Jin armies were unable to control the Jiangnan region, where there was strong resistance by the Chinese people. But the Southern Song court was satisfied with the status quo in the south, with no intention to reclaim its northern territories. In 1141 (11th year of the Shaoxing reign), a treaty was signed between the Jin and Southern Song dynasties, drawing up a new boundary along the Huaishui River in the east and Dasan Pass in the west, with the southern territories remaining in Song control, while the Jin took the northern areas. A yearly tribute was to be paid to the Jin by the Southern Song. Though the humiliating Treaty of Shaoxing put the Southern Song in a subservient position, it still maintained a period of peace for 20 years with the Jin Dynasty.

● Lu You (1125-1210), a poet of the Southern Song Dynasty, was born in Shaoxing, Zhejiang. He was deeply influenced by his father's patriotism, and thus dedicated his entire life to the mission of resisting the Jin invasion and regaining sovereignty of the Central Plains (Yellow River's mid and lower reaches); however, his political career was not smooth. As a great poet, he created more than 9,300 poems, most of which were about fighting against invasions and uniting the country. Thus, he is considered an outstanding forerunner of Southern Song poetry.

Lu You

◎ 1147-1149: The Second Crusade.

1164

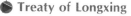

● **Zhu Xi**

● **Treaty of Longxing**

● **Lu Jiuyuan established the "School of the Mind"**

Zhu Xi

● Zhu Xi (1130-1200) was the most influential thinker and educator of the Southern Song Dynasty. His greatest contribution to Chinese philosophy was the synthesis and systematization of all fundamental Neo-Confucian concepts. Zhu Xi maintained that all things are brought into being by the union of two universal aspects of reality: *qi*, vital force; and *li*, rational principle (or law). *Qi* changes accordint to *li* and generates in the process substantial entities. He also urged to abandon human desire and abide by *tianli* (heavenly principle or law), and advised that one should study the *li* of everything in order to reach *tianli*.

● Despite the Treaty of Shaoxing, hostilities later erupted again between the Southern Song and Jin dynasties. In 1163 (1st year of the Longxing reign), the Song court launched an expedition north to attack the Jin territories, but lost the war. In 1164 a new treaty was signed between the two, which shifted the tributary state of Song into a state of subservient kinship. The boundaries stipulated in the Treaty of Shaoxing remained unchanged. The yearly tribute by the Song was reduced from originally 250,000 to 200,000 taels of silver and the same amount in silk bolts. The Treaty of Longxing extended peace between the two countries for another 40 years.

Lu Jiuyuan

● Lu Jiuyuan (1139-1193) was a townsman of Zhu Xi, but disagreed with his philosophy. In his academic debates with Zhu Xi, Lu clarified his metaphysics: Things do not exist apart from the mind, since the mind is the original source of everything in the universe, and the purpose of learning is to exert the mind in order to fully comprehend *li*. Since humans are vulnerable to material temptations, which will handicap one's mind to comprehend *li*, one should practice self-cultivation and study with teachers and friends so as to restore the mind to its purity.

© 1187-1569: Republic of Florence in Italy.

Xin Qiji

Ma Yuan

Factional persecution of the Qingyuan reign (1197-1202)

Xin Qiji (1140-1207) was born in Licheng, Jinan, and at the age of 21 called upon the people to fight the Jurchens. Shortly after that, he served the Southern Song Dynasty. Many times he made appeals to the imperial court, asking it to train its military forces, fight the Jurchen invaders and regain the lost territory. However, he was repeatedly framed and demoted. In the end, he died in grief. His long political life and social experience contributed to his patriotic, powerful style of poetry. He was the most productive and innovative *ci* poet of the Song Dynasty.

Walking and Singing

Ma Yuan (*c.* 1140-1225) was known for his landscapes. His lyrical and imaginative interpretations of landscape are defined as "fragmental mountains and rivers," since he often placed the main motif in a corner of the painting, leaving the rest of the space as if shrouded in mists or clouds that revealed no more than a fraction of a mountain or a river, or the space was simply left blank.

Upon his enthronement in 1194, Song Emperor Ningzong (r. 1194-1224) promoted his clansman Zhao Ruyu (1140-1190) and a consort clansman Han Tuozhou (1152-1207) to high positions. The two being at odds with each other, Han slandered Zhao with false charges in 1195, the first year of the Qingyuan reign. Zhao was demoted, as was the famed personage Zhu Xi, the leading figure in the Song rationalist School of Principle. Han banned rationalist writings, denouncing it as "pseudo-philosophy." Examinees who touched upon rationalist issues in the imperial examinations would be failed without exception. In 1197, Han further slandered 59 people as factional underlings of Zhao and Zhu. Han's persecution of rationalists, known as the "factional persecution of the Qingyuan reign," lasted for six years, until 1202.

○ 1189-1192: The Third Crusade.

○ 1192: Japanese shogun (military rank and historical title) Minamoto no Yoritomo(1147-1199) set up the first *bakufu* (meaning tent government, or shogunate in English) in Kamakura, known historically as the Kamakura Shogunate (-1333). *Bakufu* politics started in Japan from then on until 1867.

Genghis Khan (r. 1206-1227)

Portrait of
Genghis Khan

Genghis Khan (1162-1227), born Temüjin, was the forefather of the Mongols. In 1206, he came to power and became Khan (ruler) after uniting different Mongol tribes. He established the Mongol Empire, and took on the new title "Genghis Khan" for himself. Then he instituted military, political and legislative systems, and started to use written Mongolian language, greatly promoting the empire's social, economic and cutlural development. Beginning in 1205, Genghis Khan launched three attacks against the Western Xia and two against the Jin Dynasty. In 1215, he captured the Jin capital Zhongdu, hence establishing his authority over China's northern territory.

In 1226, he launched another war against the Western Xia Kingdom; the following year, he died in his temporary palace at the foot of Liupan Mountain in Gansu.

Mongolian Cavalry in Battle

Yelü Chucai in the service of Mongol emperors (1231-1244)

Yelü Chucai (1190-1244), of Khitan nationality with royal lineage, was well versed in astronomy, geography, calendric systems and mathematics. After Ögedei (r. 1227-1241) became Khan, Yelü was appointed chancellor (*zhongshuling*). He then helped to institute imperial protocol and formalities to honor the emperor. He made several administrative reforms, including forbidding the transformation of fields into pastureland, introducing numerous taxes and levies, and setting up official titles to manage finances and food. He also convinced the Mongolian rulers to tax and utilize rather than slaughter conquered peoples, to promote education and Confucianism, to select talented people through imperial examinations, and to set free enslaved Han Confucians. In his 13 years of tenure, he played an active role in stabilizing the Mongol empire and uniting the country.

○ 1202-1204: The Fourth Crusade; the Latin Empire was established.

○ 1206-1526: The Delhi Sultanate period in India.

○ 1215: Cruel British King John was forced to agree to the *Magna Carta* (Latin for "Great Charter") by some important barons. This charter stipulated that, without legal process, the king could not imprison people. This is the earliest form of a constitution in Britain, and in the world.

○ 1225-1400: The Tran Dynasty of Vietnam.

● Song Ci's *Collected Cases of Injustice Rectified*

A page from *Collected Cases of Injustice Rectified*

● Song Ci (1186-1249) served as a high-court presiding judge for many terms in Guangdong, Jiangxi and Hunan during the Southern Song Dynasty. He combined many historical cases of forensic science with his own experiences, and in 1247 wrote the first book on forensic science in the world, *Collected Cases of Injustice Rectified* (*Xi Yuan Ji Lu*). The book consisted of five volumes and summarized each dynastic government's actual experiences in investigating crimes. The book was held esteem by generations of forensic scientists, becoming a compulsory reference book.

● The emergence of firearms

● In 1259, a type of tube-like firearm, the "fire-shooting spear (*tuhuoqiang*)," appeared in the Southern Song army of Anhui. It was made by loading gunpowder and "bullets" (mix of porcelain, stone and iron particles) in a thick bamboo tube. When the fuse was ignited, explosion of gunpowder produced powerful pressure inside the bamboo tube, and the "bullets" shot out with a loud noise. The shooting range could reach about 230 m. As bamboo easily burned, it was later replaced by metal.

Sketch of a fire-shooting spear

● China's economic center moved south

● From the 8th century onwards, northern China was harassed by constant warfare, thus causing large-scale southward migrations. The south therefore received a wealth of labor and advanced technology. In the early 12th century, the political center moved to the Yangtze River drainage area. Therefore, from the Southern Song Dynasty onwards, southern China became much more developed agriculturally and commercially, compared to northern China. For instance, Jiangsu and Zhejiang's agricultural products were able to serve the entire country. Moreover, southern commercial activities and foreign trade were much more prosperous than that of the north.

© Saint Thomas Aquinas (1225-1274), Italian philosopher and theologian in the scholastic tradition, wrote the book *Summa Theologica*. His book accomplished the Christian theological system and created the theory of "royal god-given rights."

© 1265: First Parliament of England held.

Yuan Dynasty ● Kublai Khan (r. 1271-1294)

● In 1260 Kublai succeeded the Khan of the Mongol Empire; in 1271 he changed the dynasty title to "Yuan," and the following year had the capital moved to Dadu. In 1279 the Yuan eliminated the Southern Song Dynasty and united China. The Yuan central bureaucracy included Zhong Shu Sheng, Shu Mi Yuan and Yu Shi Tai, respectively taking charge of government affairs, military affairs and supervision work. Except for a few regions directly under the central government, the entire country was divided into different administrative provinces. During this dynasty, irrigation works, agriculture and handicraft were greatly developed; post stations were set up at important land and water passageways; transportation was improved; and the economy, culture and foreign trade were also extensively developed. However, domestic policy also retained aspects of old Mongol traditions, and as its rule continued, these traditions clashed more and more frequently with traditional Chinese economic, social and cultural values. After it was established by Kublai Khan, the Yuan Dynasty went through 11 emperors, until eventually expelled by Ming forces to the Mongolian Plateau in 1368.

Yuan Mongols' Autumn Hunting Expedition (detail)

Portrait of Kublai Khan

● Kublai Khan (1215-1294), Genghis Khan's grandson, became Khan in 1260. In 1271, he called his empire "Yuan," and himself "Emperor," following Han tradition. Soon he launched a large-scale attack on the Southern Song Dynasty and conquered it in 1279, marking the unification of China under his rule. Kublai Khan paid great attention to the Han people's culture and followed their political organizations and systems. He also divided China into different administrative provinces, the origins of modern provinces. Kublai Khan died in 1294, and was given the posthumous name Yuan Shizu.

© Dante (1265-1321), forerunner of the Italian Renaissance and creator of *Divine Comedy*.

Phagpa

Phagpa (1235/1239-1280) was the fifth leader of the Sakya Sect of Tibetan Buddhism. In 1260, Kublai Khan made him "State Preceptor" and gave him a jade seal and power to govern Buddhist affairs in China. In 1264, Kublai Khan appointed him head of Zong Zhi Yuan (predecessor of Xuan Zheng Yuan, or Commission for Buddhist and Tibetan Affairs). In 1269 Phagpa created a new Mongolian writing system, which was implemented across the country. In 1276, he returned to Tibet and established himself as the first Dharma King of the Sakya Temple. He assisted the Yuan central government to rule Tibet. He also brought Tibetan Buddhist arts into the Central Plains area, contributing to cultural exchange between the Han and Tibetan people.

Phagba

Guan Hanqing

Facsimile of *The Injustice Suffered by Dou E*

Guan Hanqing (*c.* 1230-1300), a great playwright in the 13th century, produced 67 plays in total, and 20 of them have survived, including the most famous *The Injustice Suffered by Dou E* (*Dou E Yuan*), *The Jade Mirror Dresser* (*Yujing Tai*) and *Saving a Prostitute* (*Jiu Fengchen*). With profound themes and critical insights, Guan's works revolved around the underside of society and corrupt officials of that time. His great success in characterization, dramatic conflicts and theatric language has made him popular throughout the following centuries. His works have also been introduced to other countries.

Gong Kai

Gong Kai (1222-1307) spanned the Song and Yuan dynasties. His paintings, which covered a wide range of topics, were created in a unique style of composition and brushwork. His representative work, *Emaciated Horse* (*Shou Ma Tu*) depicts the spare beauty and mightiness of a swift horse, its head lowered, and ribs clearly visible. Another painting, *Zhong Kui from Zhongshan on a Journey* (*Zhongshan Chuyou Tu*) depicts Zhong Kui traveling. The inscription on the painting suggests that the artist wanted Zhong Kui to catch "ghosts" (Mongol rulers). It reveals the artist's melancholy and dissatisfaction over Mongol rule of China.

Emaciated Horse

© Italian painter Giotto di Bondone (1267-1337) introduced the realist style of painting to Italy. His representative works include *Last Judgment* and *Kiss of Judas*.

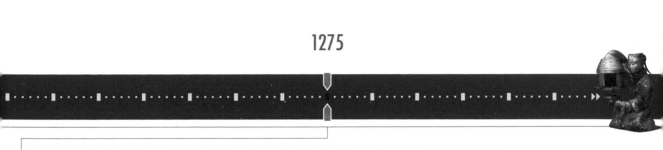

● **Marco Polo in China** ● **Wen Tianxiang fought the Yuan Dynasty (1275-1283)**

● In 1275 Marco Polo (1254-1324), a 21-year-old Venetian merchant, followed his father to the Yuan capital Dadu and visited Kublai Khan. He thus started his 17-year stay including journeys through China and neighboring areas. In 1298, the third year after returning home, Marco Polo was captured during a minor clash in a war between Venice and Genoa. In prison, he finished his world-famous book, *The Travels of Marco Polo*. This book gave a vivid, detailed account of politics, society, customs, religions, local products and interesting tales of China and other Asian countries. It presented an enchanting Chinese culture that aroused great European interest in the East.

Wen Tianxiang

● Wen Tianxiang (1236-1283), was a native of Luling, Jizhou (now Ji'an, Jiangxi Province). In 1275, the Yuan armies crossed the Yangtze River and threatened Lin'an, capital of the Southern Song Dynasty. Wen sold all his property, and recruited some 10,000 men to defend the throne. When the enemies reached the city gate of Lin'an in 1276, Wen was appointed as Prime Minister to negotiate with the Yuan, but was imprisoned. After escaping, he continued fighting Yuan forces in Guangdong. In 1278, he was captured in Guangdong, but he refused to surrender and wrote *Song of Righteousness* (*Zhengqi Ge*), with the famous lines, "None since the advent of time have escaped death, may my loyalty forever illuminate the annals of history." He is considered one of the greatest examples of patriotism in Chinese history.

Marco Polo

© 1273-1806: The ruling period of the Habsburg family in the Holy Roman Empire.

Quanzhou and the "Maritime Silk Road"

Guo Shoujing

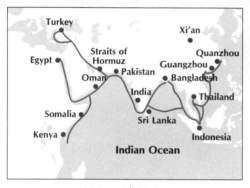

Maritime Silk Route

In the 13th century, the Southern Song Dynasty's maritime trade was already relatively mature. A navigation route that mainly traded in Chinese silk, ceramics and Indian spices had been formed, commonly known as the "Maritime Silk Road." It ran through the Indian Ocean to countries along the Persian Gulf. Quanzhou, a harbor city on the southeast coast of China, was known to be the "start of the Maritime Silk Road" and "No. 1 Harbor in the Orient." Even during the Yuan Dynasty, it retained its status. There were more than 100 countries and regions trading with the Yuan, including Japan, Koryo (now Korea) and some Eastern African countries. The Yuan government specially established an office in Quanzhou to preside over maritime trade. As more and more merchants came to Quanzhou for trade, its culture grew more diversified. Even today, visitors to Quanzhou can see traces of once prosperous Islam, Nestorianism, Manichaeism, Catholicism, Christianity and Buddhism.

In 1279, the astronomer Guo Shoujing (1231-1316) devised a number of astronomical instruments, including the armillary sphere and celestial body, and used them to conduct a series of large-scale geodetic surveys and celestial observations in 27 places in China. According to the results of his observations, Guo formulated the Shoushi Calendar, which became the most advanced calendar of that time, and used for the longest time. He calculated a solar year to be 365.2425 days, the same as the Gregorian calendar.

Model of Guo's abridged armilla

© Late 13th century: Handicraft guilds sprouted in Western Europe.
© 1283: Principality of Moscow established.

Wang Shifu and his *Romance of the Western Chamber*

Facsimile of Romance of the Western Chamber

Wang Shifu (birth and death dates unknown) was a Yuan playwright, born a little later than Guan Hanqing. Fourteen of his plays have survived, including the famous *Romance of the Western Chamber*. This play tells the love story of a young scholar from a poor family and the daughter of a high-ranking official and how they pursued love in defiance of the social hierarchal barrier. The play is celebrated for its intriguing story line, beautiful language, and masterly characterization.

Huang Daopo innovated textile technology

In 1295, an ordinary woman named Huang Daopo brought back to her hometown Songjiang (now in Shanghai) the more advanced textile technology that she had learned from the Li people in Hainan. She innovated textile tools and designed new cotton gins, spinning wheels and looms that enhanced production efficiency by leaps and bounds. She also taught the local women advanced weaving skills greatly improving the texture and pattern diversity of fabrics. By the 14th century, cotton cultivation was introduced to most of the southern areas in China, and Songjiang became the biggest textile center in China.

Huang Daopo's weaving method

Zhao Mengfu

Autumn Colors on the Que and Hua Mountains (detail)

Zhao Mengfu (1254-1322) was a calligrapher and artist of the Yuan Dynasty. He was well versed in the calligraphy of round hand (*zhengkai*), running hand (*xingshu*) and regular script (*xiaokai*). His calligraphy featured roundness and vitality. He was known for his landscape paintings, said to use a style that incorporated calligraphy techniques. He was in favor of the crude and substantial style of the Tang Dynasty. His representative work, *Autumn Colors on the Que and Hua Mountains* (*Que Hua Qiuse Tu*), 28.4 x 93 cm, depicts scenery outside of Jinan, in Shandong.

◎ At the end of the 13th century, the Florentine School developed in Italy, including almost all the important painters during the Renaissance.
◎ 13th-17th centuries: The Renaissance in Europe.

Provincial administration system

During the Yuan Dynasty, the central government set up Zhong Shu Sheng (central administration) and 11 provincial administrations, including Henan (now part of Henan, Jiangsu, Anhui and Hubei), Huguang (now Hunan and part of Guangdong, Guangxi and Hubei), Jiangzhe (now Fujian, Zhejiang and part of Jiangsu, Anhui and Jiangxi) and Gansu (now part of Gansu, Qinghai, Ningxia, Inner Mongolia and Xinjiang). The provincial administrations took charge of local affairs on behalf of the central administration. This administrative system marked the start of China's provinces and has been passed down to the present day.

Comprehensive Examination of Literature

Comprehensive Examination of Literature is a general historical record of rituals and institutional establishments in China from primeval times to the reign of Song Emperor Ningzong (r. 1194-1224). Allegedly compiled around 1307, the book is divided into 24 categories, with a further 348 volumes. In addition to the official histories of past dynasties, the book also included relevant records from personal writings, to present clearer accounts of various institutional establishments. Featuring detailed records of the Song Dynasty, the book was also original in its interpretations of the changing institutional orders of different dynasties.

Huang Gongwang

Huang Gongwang (1269-1354), a Yuan artist native to Jiangsu, started to create landscape paintings in his 50s. He often went to visit Mount Yu and Fuchun River, and painted the beautiful scenery there. He liked to do ink-wash, added with reddish hues. His brushwork was simple, elegant and powerful, greatly influencing the painting of later generations. Some of his works have survived to the present day, such as *Dwelling in the Fuchun Mountains (Fuchunshan Ju Tu)* and *Streams and Mountains in Rain (Xi Shan Yuyi Tu)*.

Dwelling in the Fuchun Mountains (detail)

○ 1299: Osman I established the Ottoman Empire.

○ 1302: The States-General (*états généraux*, a legislative assembly of the different classes of French subjects) was held for the first time in France.

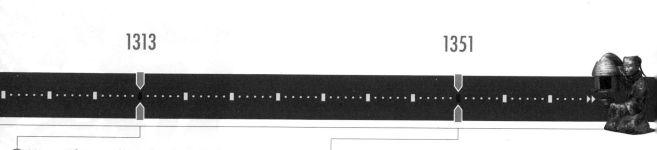

Wang Zhen and *Book of Agriculture*

Red Turban Rebellion (1351-1368)

Illustration of a spinning wheel,
from *Book of Agriculture*

Nong Shu (*Book of Agriculture*), written by Wang Zhen (*c.* 1271-1330), a Yuan scientist, is a comprehensive book about agriculture. Published in 1313, it consists of three parts totaling over 130,000 words: the first, Comprehensive Prescriptions for Agriculture and Sericulture (six chapters) records the author's agricultural theories; the second, Treatise on the Hundred Grains (11 chapters) details the cultivating technologies of crops, vegetables and fruits; and the third, Illustrated Treatise on Agricultural Implements (20 chapters), accounting for 80 percent of the entire book, introduces almost all traditional agricultural tools and facilities. As the earliest illustrated agricultural book in China, it has been used by later generations as a reference book for agricultural work.

At the end of the Yuan Dynasty, people had to endure heavy taxes and corvee, resulting in intense social conflicts igniting the wrath of the peasantry. In 1351, peasants were organized into a revolutionary army by the White Lotus (Buddhist sect). The appellation "Red Turban" was used because of their tradition of using red banners and wearing red turbans to distinguish themselves. This rebellion gave Yuan rule a heavy jolt, and also gave rise to the founder of the Ming, Zhu Yuanzhang, who annihilated the Yuan Dynasty after about ten years.

The White Lotus

The White Lotus was a mysterious Buddhist sect that appealed to many Chinese, starting in the Song and becoming popular in the Yuan Dynasty. It incorporated Confucian, Taoist and Buddhist theories and worshipped the future Buddha Maitreya. It adhered to the five commandments of "no killing, no stealing, no cheating, no rumor-mongering, and no drinking." Most of its adherents came from the lower classes.

◎ 1323: Italian poet Francesco Petrarca (1304-1374) published his collection of poems, *Canzoniere* (*Song Book*), which blazed a new trail for European romantic poetry.

◎ Giovanni Boccaccio (1313-1375), Italian writer, poet, and author of the humanist classic, *Decameron*.

◎ 1336-1562: The Muromachi Era in Japan.

◎ 1347-1353: The plague or "Black Death" spread in Europe, with total number of deaths estimated at 24 million.

1368 - 1644

Ming Dynasty ● Zhu Yuanzhang (r. 1368-1398)

● The Ming became the last dynasty of the Han people in Chinese history. It spanned over 227 years, with 17 emperors. During a history of more than two centuries, China made great achievements in its economy, culture, science and technology. Massive amounts of silver were brought in and capital flourished, clearly influencing the world economy. The Ming era witnessed the rise of popular literature, represented by *Outlaws of the Marsh*, *Romance of the Three Kingdoms*, *Journey to the West*, and *The Golden Lotus*. Up until the 16th century, China's science and technology still took the lead in the world, and many technological inventions emerged, as well as some science books. During the early Ming, the government applied a fairly open foreign policy, but after mid-dynasty it became more and more conservative. A political phenomenon unique to the Ming Dynasty emerged, with the emperor sanctioning eunuchs and granting them excessive rights over civil bureaucracy. In 1644, the Ming Dynasty was overthrown after Li Zicheng's peasant force captured Beijing.

Zhu Yuanzhang

● During the Red Turban Rebellion, which had religious characteristics, Zhu Yuanzhang [1328-1398], born to a peasant's family and later a monk, rose rapidly to attain high stature due to his extraordinary talent. In 1356, Zhu sacked Nanjing and amassed forces there. He then defied the Red Turban Army and called it an "evil spirit." He eliminated other anti-Yuan forces and headed north to conquer the Yuan Dynasty. In 1368, Zhu Yuanzhang was enthroned, deciding the dynasty title should be "Ming" (Brightness) and his reigning title "Hongwu" (Almighty), and basing the capital in Nanjing. In August of that year, Ming forces occupied Dadu, announcing the Yuan's end.

Metropolitan Prosperity of Southern Capital (detail)

Shi Nai'an and *Outlaws of the Marsh*

Luo Guanzhong and *Romance of the Three Kingdoms*

Shi Nai'an (?-1370), a Ming Dynasty novelist, created one of the four greatest Chinese classics, *Outlaws of the Marsh*. It recounts, in chapters, the story of 108 outlaws at Mount Liang, who resisted the corrupt Song Dynasty government. These are stories of courage, bravery, intrigue, murder, and triumph over oppression, corruption and forces of evil. This novel successfully modeled many flamboyant characters including Song Jiang, Wu Song, Li Kui and Lu Zhishen. With a lively style of writing and intriguing plots, this classic has very high literary value.

Facsimile of *Romance
of the Three Kingdoms*

Luo Guanzhong (?-1400) was a novelist writing at the end of the Yuan Dynasty. The *Romance of the Three Kingdoms* is his historical novel of many chapters. It revolves around the conflicts and battles between the three political and military states of Wei, Shu and Wu, during the turbulent years of the 3rd century. The book depicts political and military strife, as well as the strategies unique to that era, with a far-reaching impact on later generations. As one of the four greatest Chinese classics, *Romance of the Three Kingdoms* presents readers with many widely known characters including Zhuge Liang, Guan Yunchang and Cao Cao.

Characters from *Outlaws of the Marsh*

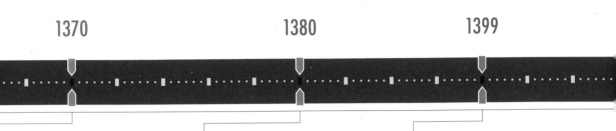
▶ **China started the census**   ▶ **The Case of Hu Weiyong**   ▶ **Jingnan Rebellion (1399-1402)**

Portrait of Zhu Di

A Residents' Book from Jiangshou, Qimen County, Huizhou

▶ In November 1370, the founder of the Ming Dynasty, Zhu Yuanzhang sent troops to assist local governments to conduct a nationwide census. Every household was given a residents' book, which recorded the house owner's name, birthplace and family members, with detailed information including names, gender, age, and relationship to the owner. After registration was completed, all residents' books were kept by the Board of Revenue and Population of the central government. Every year, each region had to report an updated count of the population, so as to calculate more accurate overall demographics of the nation.

▶ Hu Weiyong (?-1380) was an early follower of Zhu Yuanzhang, or Emperor Hongwu, and as an intimate of the emperor was promoted to the senior position of Chancellor of the Left. The powerful Hu became corrupt, banding together underlings to dominate the court. In 1380, Emperor Hongwu had him executed for infringing on imperial sovereignty. After this lesson, the emperor abrogated the position of Chancellor, dismissed the Zhong Shu Sheng, and divided power among the Six Ministries. The chancellor system thereafter ended its 1,000-year exercise.

▶ The second emperor of the Ming Dynasty was Zhu Yunwen, the first Ming emperor Zhu Yuanzhang's eldest grandson. He conspired with his officials to abolish the princedoms, so as to undermine his uncles' power. In this situation, Prince of the Yan, Zhu Di began to plan rebellion. In 1399, Zhu Di led his army from northern China to the south, and captured Nanjing in 1402, replacing Zhu Yunwen as the new emperor, known in history by his posthumous title as Emperor Chengzu. This usurpation of the throne is known in history as the "Jingnan Rebellion."

Imperial Court's secret service

Yongle Encyclopedia
(1403-1408)

During the Ming Dynasty, emperors gave unprecedented power to eunuchs and bodyguards who were the emperors' eyes and ears. They were organized into a secret-service department called "Changwei," which oversaw the conduct of the general populace as well as civil and military officials. They could arrest and punish suspects (including officials and imperial family members). These corrupt eunuchs and bodyguards abused their power, took bribes, and were allowed to persecute, imprison and torture suspects to death without due process.

Merry eunuchs, in *Emperor Xianzong Enjoying the Lantern Festival*

The Changwei secret-service department of the imperial court, unique to the Ming Dynasty, consisted of three major organizations. The first was the secret police (Jingyiwei) organized by the first Ming emperor; as the emperor's bodyguards, they had the power to bypass judicial procedures and were in charge of arresting, imprisoning and punishing people. The second, the Eastern Yard (Dongchang) was established by Ming Emperor Chengzu in 1420, to spy on the capital city proper; it was controlled by eunuchs and subject to the emperor. The third, the Western Yard (Xichang) was established by Emperor Xianzong in 1477 and expanded surveillance to outside of Beijing; its official positions were all taken up by eunuchs.

Facsimile of
Yongle Encyclopedia

The *Yongle Encyclopedia* was a Chinese compilation commissioned by Ming Emperor Chengzu between the first and sixth year (1403-1408) of the Yongle Reign. The entire encyclopedia systematically incorporated 8,000 books and writings from pre-Qin up to the early Ming Dynasty, in 22,877 volumes. This covered an array of subjects, including philosophy, history, geography, language, literature, art, religion, science and technology.

Zheng He's voyages to the Western Seas (1405-1433)

In the early Ming Dynasty, with state support, the eunuch general Zheng He sailed to the "Western Seas" (westward beyond the South China Sea) seven times from 1405 to 1433, traveling to India, Africa and the Middle East. On each journey he led more than 100 ships with 28,000 companions, and took abroad Chinese porcelain, bronze, iron, silver and gold wares, as well as exquisite silk products. At the same time, he brought back many special products from other Asian and African countries, including pepper, ivory, gems, dyes, medicine, spices, and rare animals such as giraffes, lions, ostriches and leopards. His seven voyages greatly promoted China's trade with other Asian and African countries.

Model of Zheng He's ship

The Ming constructed the Forbidden City (1407-1420)

The Forbidden City, an early Ming painting of the palace

After Ming Emperor Chengzu came to power, he decided to have the capital moved to Beijing and started the construction of the imperial residence. Completed in 1420, the Forbidden City became home to 24 emperors and administrations of the Ming and Qing dynasties over some 500 years. Covering a total area of 720,000 sq m, with a floor space of 150,000 sq m, the entire palace consists of more than 9,000 bays of rooms within a 3 km palace wall. The symmetrical palace complex sits on a south-north axis, with the imperial court in the front and the living quarters at the back. As the largest and best-preserved ancient palace complex in the world, it exemplifies traditional Chinese palace architecture symbolizing the supreme power of the emperor.

1449

The "Tumu Crisis"

In 1449, the Wala tribe (Oirat Mongols) invaded the Ming's northern frontier. The eunuch official Wang Zhen, who dominated the Ming court, encouraged the emperor to lead his own armies into battle against the Mongols. The result was the Ming armies' defeat at the post station of Tumu, with the emperor captured and Wang Zhen killed in chaos. This event is called the "Tumu Crisis."

A eunuch official of the Ming Dynasty

The "Eight-Legged Essay" became standard in imperial examinations

Founded in the Sui Dynasty, the Imperial Examination System had been in place for about 1,000 years when some disappointing changes took place in the mid-Ming Dynasty. Both the test content and the essay writing style became subject to rigid formulations. First, the topics had to be from the "Four Books." Second, the answers had to conform to the philosophic school of rationalist Neo-Confucianism, and the interpretations of Confucian classics by the Cheng brothers and Zhu Xi. Third, a rigid structure was stipulated for essay writing, known as the "eight-legged" or "eight-part" essay," with introduction, exposition, argumentation and conclusion, each in two sections. Even the number of sentences was specified for each part.

Tang Bohu

Lady Holding a Fan in Autumn Breeze (detail)

Tang Yin (1470-1523), styled Bohu, was a well-known Ming artist. His landscapes feature stunningly steep mountains, ranging and towering, depicted by the light use of ink in an elegantly clear style. For figure painting, Tang preferred to paint beautiful women as well as historical tales. With the mastery of his fine-brush skills, he breathed life into the figures with graceful bearings, simple yet elegant. When it came to flowers and birds, Tang's freehand style of ink and wash imbued his subjects with a leisurely beauty.

◎ Italian artist Leonardo da Vinci (1452-1519), outstanding representative of the Renaissance, created many works including *Mona Lisa* and *Last Supper*.

◎ During the Renaissance, Michelangelo (1475-1564) pushed sculptural arts to its zenith, with his *Dying Slave*, *Rebellious Slave*, *Moses*, and other works.

◎ Raphael (1483-1520), one of the three prominent painters during the Renaissance, created *Sistine Madonna*, *The School of Athens*, and other classics.

Wen Zhengming

Wang Yangming

Yan Song, the Prime Minister

▶ Wen Zhengming (1470-1559), a Ming artist and calligrapher from an official's family, was accomplished in poetry and essay writing, as well as in calligraphy and painting. Acknowledged as the founder of the "Wumen School" of painting, Wen's works touched a variety of subjects: landscapes, figures, flowers, orchids, and bamboo, among many others. With fine-brush techniques and the use of light colors, serene compositions were conceived in his well laid-out landscapes. Human figures also were often casually painted in isolation to bring about a feeling of internal strength. Wen's main works include *Mountain and River Landscape* and *Spring in Jiangnan*.

Portrait of
Wang Yangming

▶ Wang Yangming (1472-1529), also known as Shouren, was an important figure in the history of Chinese philosophy. He systemized Lu Jiuyuan's *Xinxue* (the School of the Mind), and developed it into a new philosophy opposing the then-prevailing *Lixue* (the Study of Principle). He believed that "objects do not exist apart from the mind," and that "the mind gives birth to all." He further argued that the mind was the primary source of the universe, without which the world would not exist. With profound and far-reaching influence in China, the School of the Mind also affected idealist thinking abroad.

▶ The organization known as the "Cabinet" emerged in the Ming Dynasty, at first a mere secretarial branch. Later, the branch developed with more officials holding important positions, and finally served as a body with executive power representing the emperor. Yan Song (1480-1567), promoted to Prime Minister in 1544 by Emperor Jiajing, controlled the court for almost 20 years. The corrupt Yan persecuted and killed righteous officials, while banding together his own underlings to consolidate his status. Under him, the nation saw no hope, in an era of moral decadence and corruption.

Portrait of Yan Song

Mountain and River landscape

◎ 1488: Portuguese explorer Bartolomeu Dias (1450-1500) reached the Cape of Good Hope, the southernmost point of Africa.
◎ 1492-1504: Christopher Columbus (1451-1506), on his fourth voyage, came upon the Americas.
◎ 1517: Martin Luther (1483-1546) inspired Protestantism through religious reforms.
◎ 1519-1522: Ferdinand Magellan (1480-1521) led the first maritime expedition around the world.

Portugal occupied Macao
Battles against Japanese pirates led by Qi Jiguang (1553-1567)

Portuguese traders landed in Macao in 1553, on the excuse of needing to dry out drenched goods. After bribing local officials, they were granted rights of habitation. Along the coastal regions of what is now Nam Van, the traders built houses, set up emplacements, and constructed fortresses with watchtowers. As a settlement of the Portuguese, Macao developed into the first trade port connecting the West and the East, where new cultures and religions were flourishing. Following the Opium War, Portugal occupied Taipa in 1851, then Coloane in 1864. After almost 450 years of foreign occupation, the Chinese government finally resumed sovereignty over Macao in 1999.

Painting scroll of Qi Jiguang's battles against the *wokou* (detail)

The *wokou* were actually a gang of pirates, including Japanese samurai, vagabonds, bandits, sailors, buccaneers, and their Chinese counterparts. During the period between the 14th and 16th centuries, the *wokou* constantly raided the coastlines of China. Without a strong naval force, the Ming government had no choice but to ban maritime trade. In 1553, Qi Jiguang (1528-1587), a renowned military commander, was sent to Zhejiang by the Ming government to fight off the pirates. Qi drafted miners and farmers, and trained them into an elite force. With his powerful army, Qi eliminated the pirates in Taizhou Prefecture in 1561. Following the victory, he led his armies south to Fujian and Guangdong, and finally eradicated the *wokou* in 1567. Maritime trade was resumed shortly after.

A 19th century oil painting of Macao scenery

○ 1526-1858: The Mughal Empire in ancient India.
○ 1541: John Calvin (1509-1564) pushed religious reforms in Geneva during the Protestant Reformation.
○ 1543: Polish astronomer Copernicusn (1473-1543) finished his magnum opus, *On the Revolutions of the Celestial Spheres*, proposing the Heliocentric Model.

Altan Khan and Lady Sanniangzi

Wu Cheng'en and *Journey to the West*

Portrait of
Lady Sanniangzi

Altan Khan (1507-1581) was the ruler of the Tumed Mongols in the late Ming Dynasty. After years of development, he transformed his khanate into a political, cultural and economic center of the Mongol territory. Lady Sanniangzi (1550-1612), who married Altan Khan as his "third wife" (literal meaning of Sanniangzi), was from the Torgout tribe of the Mongols. With her intelligence and talent, Lady Sanniangzi assisted her husband to govern, and after Altan Khan's death, actually ruled for over 30 years. During her leadership, the Tumed Mongols continued to thrive as a unified country. She was loved by both Mongols and Han people for her contributions to lasting peace between the two nationalities.

In the first half of the 16th century (c. 1570), drawing on folklore, drama and ghost stories, Wu Cheng'en (1500-1582) exercised great imagination and composed *Journey to the West*, a classic mythical novel enjoyed by generations of Chinese. Grounded in the true historical event of Tang monk Xuanzang's pilgrimage to India in search of Buddhist scriptures, Wu created an imaginative world of gods and ghosts for the monk and his disciples to explore. The enduring popularity of the novel could be attributed to its dramatic and fantastic plots, humorous language, as well as its successful depiction of the main characters Sun Wukong (Monkey King) and Zhu Bajie (Pigsy). As one of the Four Great Classical Novels, *Journey to the West* occupies an important position in Chinese literature.

Picture book *Journey to the West*

© 1566: The Bourgeois Revolution broke out in the Netherlands. In 1648, Holland was recognized as an independent nation by European countries.

Zhang Juzheng's reforms (1573-1582)

Li Shizhen's *Compendium of Materia Medica*

Zhang Juzheng

In the last three decades of the 16th century, the Ming Dynasty oversaw an almost exhausted national treasury. Zhang Juzheng (1525-1582), as Chief of the Cabinet, spent 10 years enriching the imperial treasury and the granary. A series of wide-ranging reforms were enacted. In administration, Zhang rectified misconduct in government, and regulated the activities of officials. In military affairs, he sent Qi Jiguang and other generals to defend the northern frontier. In agriculture, he took flood control measures to regulate the Yellow and Huaihe rivers. He also encouraged land reclamation, and collected taxes according to land area. However, after his death in 1582, Zhang's policies were slowly abolished, and his deeds slandered.

Facsimile of *Bencao Gangmu*

Born to a family of doctors, Li Shizhen (1518-1593) was one of the greatest physicians and pharmacologists in Chinese history. In the 27-year writing of the *Bencao Gangmu* (*Compendium of Materia Medica*), he traveled extensively, gaining firsthand experience using various herbs and local remedies, and consulted over 800 books. Totaling over 900,000 characters, the grand work details about 1,892 Chinese medicines, 374 discovered for the first time, together with 11,096 prescriptions and 1,160 illustrations. As a systemic summary of previous achievements in Chinese medicine, Li's book also made a great contribution to the study of zoology, botany, and mineralogical chemistry. In 1606, the book was introduced to Japan, and its Latin translation spread westward 40 years after.

Xu Wei

Matteo Ricci in China

Inked Grapes

Matteo Ricci (left) and
Xu Guangqi (right)

Xu Wei (1521-1593) was a Ming artist and calligrapher. As a master of the brush, Xu was especially famed for his grand free-hand-style ink-and-wash paintings of flowers and birds. In the use of ink, he combined various techniques into his paintings: splashing ink to outline the subjects, applying a different stroke of ink to blend or modify an existing image, and employing layers of ink to create depth. After conceiving the design and layout of a painting, Xu would splash and spread ink, sprinkling and dotting in different shades here and there, so as to bring to life a harmoniously blended water-ink representation of his unconstrained passion. His *Inked Grapes*, *Peony and Rockery under a Palm Tree*, and other masterpieces best reveal his artistic influence on later painters.

In 1582, Matteo Ricci (1552-1610), an Italian missionary, journeyed to China to proselytize during the Wanli Reign of the Ming Dynasty. To accomplish his mission, Ricci learned the Chinese language, along with the culture and customs. In 1601, he arrived in Beijing, and presented the Emperor with Christian writings, icons of Christ, a chiming clock and a piano. He made wide acquaintance with Chinese officials and eminent figures, spreading knowledge of astronomy, mathematics, geography, and other Western sciences. Later, he obtained imperial permission to stay and preach, and was granted an official post. After his death, Ricci was buried outside Beijing's Xizhimen.

▶ Nurhachi

Portrait of Nurhachi

▶ A descendant of the Jurchen founders of the Jin Dynasty, Nurhachi (1559-1626) unified the Jurchen people through brilliant political and military maneuvers. In 1583, he rose up to fight for supremacy against the Ming Dynasty. Nurhachi ordered the creation of the written Jurchen (Manchu) language and established the "Eight Banners System," a multifunctional structure organizing the military, administration, production, and other aspects of social life. This system was a vital move towards enhancing the military prowess of the armies. In 1616, Nurhachi established the Later Jin regime, marking the start of an independent country paralleling Ming China. Led by Nurhachi, the Later Jin armies won multiple battles against the Ming armies. However, Nurhachi died of severe wounds in the campaign of Ningyuan in 1626, leaving his ambition of conquering central China for his son to accomplish.

Official seals of the leaders of
the Eight Banners

▶ Li Zhi and *Book to Burn*

Facsimile of *Book to Burn*

▶ Li Zhi (1527-1602), a Ming philosopher, held minor official posts for years, before concentrating on writing and preaching his theories in his later years. Disagreeing with the ascetic rationalist school of *Lixue* (the Study of Principle) that suppressed "human desires" with "heavenly principles," he argued that "everyday feeding and clothing of people are the substantial human principle," stressing the importance of material life. In 1590, Li published *Book to Burn* (*Fen Shu*). Seen as a heretical text, the book was indeed burned as its name suggested, and its author imprisoned. In 1602, Li committed suicide.

© English poet and playwright William Shakespeare (1564-1616) wrote the plays *Hamlet*, *Othello*, *King Lear*, *Macbeth*, *The Merchant of Venice*, and other masterpieces; and composed many famed sonnets.

Tang Xianzu and *The Peony Pavilion*

Dong Qichang

Tang Xianzu (1550-1616) was an eminent playwright of the Ming Dynasty, when drama was not so developed as in the Yuan. However, he is now widely acclaimed for his 1598 masterpiece *The Peony Pavilion*, and is even extolled as the "Shakespeare of the East." *The Peony Pavilion* tells the love story of a young couple, describing in detail how their suppressed love germinated, brewed, and finally erupted. With its vivid description of inner thoughts and feelings in lyrical language, *The Peony Pavilion* is hailed as China's Romeo and Juliet.

Mount Bian in Green,
by Dong Qichang

The Ming calligrapher and artist Dong Qichang (1555-1636) was expert in landscape painting. Absorbing the essence of traditional skills and techniques, Dong developed a simple and natural style, stressing the use of ink to create different shades and layers. He stressed the importance of learning from previous masters by "reading 10,000 books," and seeking inspiration from nature through "traveling 10,000 miles." Dong also divided artists into two schools based on their use of ink and aesthetic effects: the Southern School and the Northern School.

Facsimile of *The Peony Pavilion*

1604

Donglin Movement (1604-1644)

"Vernacular fiction"

In 1604, Gu Xiancheng, a former official with the Personnel Ministry, lectured at the Donglin Academy in Wuxi. Including local intellectuals, the Academy became a center of dissent regarding current public affairs. Donglin opposition to corrupt officials and eunuchs resulted in the torture and execution of participants, who were vilified as "Donglin partisans." The persecution continued until the accession of Emperor Chongzhen (r. 1627-1644). Yet the Donglin intellectuals went on to struggle against the eunuchs until the Manchus entered central China in 1644. The movement lasted more than 40 years.

Donglin Academy

"Pinghua," a form of storytelling performance in ancient China, developed into an important genre in Chinese literature after being recorded in written language. "Vernacular fiction" used simple language to write about the lives of ordinary people. Its target readers could find images of themselves in the ups and downs, joys and sorrows in lives of the characters. As a new writing genre, "vernacular fiction" was distinguished from classical literature by its vivid description of daily life.

San Yan (*Three Words*) and *Er Pai* (*Two Slaps*) were masterpieces of "vernacular fiction." They were short stories of the Song and Ming dynasties collected by Feng Menglong (1574-1646) and Ling Mengchu (1580-1644), respectively. *San Yan* includes *Illustrious Words to Instruct the World*, *Comprehensive Words to Caution the World*, and *Lasting Words to Awaken the World*; and *Er Pai*, *An Astonished Slap upon the Desktop* and *A Second Astonished Slap upon the Desktop*.

○ 1603-1867: Reign of Tokugawa Shogunate (General) in Japan.
○ 1605: Spanish writer Miguel de Cervantes (1547-1615) composed *Don Quixote*.

Xu Xiake's *Travel Diaries*

Publication of *The Golden Lotus*

Xu Xiake (1586-1641), born Xu Hongzu, throughout his life refused to sit for imperial examinations. Instead, he traveled extensively and devoted himself to geographical studies. For decades, Xu traveled throughout south China, carrying out scientific observations in the fields of geography, geology, hydrology, and botany. On his journeys, Xu kept a journal recording his findings, which were later compiled into *The Travel Diaries of Xu Xiake*. In the diaries, he recorded many new discoveries in geography. He proved that the Jinsha River was a headwater stream of the Yangtze River, and the Lancang (Mekong) and Nu (Salween) rivers had different headwaters. He was also credited with the first studies of the Karst topography in southwest China.

Portrait of Xu Hongzu

The year 1617 saw the publication of *The Golden Lotus*. Composed in the Ming Dynasty, *The Golden Lotus* (*Jin Ping Mei*) was a highly controversial novel in Chinese literature. It is considered the first full-length original novel, on the grounds that previous similar fictional renditions had been merely edited and modified folklore. The book was much debated on two aspects. For one, centered on the daily lives of common people, the book was highly realistic in its description and analysis of complex human relationships in a corrupt society. It eclipsed all its previous counterparts for its insight into human nature. In its other aspect, the novel contained a surprising amount of explicit sexual detail, resulting in its ban for a long time as a pornographic book.

Illustration from *The Golden Lotus*

Facsimile of *The Travel Diaries of Xu Xiake*

◎ 1607: English colonists established the first colony in Virginia.
◎ 1609: Italian scientist Galileo Galilei invented the first telescope to probe the universe.
◎ 1609: German scholar Johannes Kepler (1571-1630) noted that planets move around the sun in elliptical orbits.

▶ Johann Adam Schall von Bell came to China

▶ Dutch occupation of Taiwan

▶ Chen Hongshou

▶ Johann Adam Schall von Bell, a missionary of the German Society of Jesus, traveled to China in 1620. As an expert astronomer and mathematician, he gained his reputation by predicting a solar eclipse in 1623. Later, under imperial command, he compiled and modified the existing calendar into the Chongzhen Calendar, winning himself the name of "another Matteo Ricci." Even after the fall of the Ming Dynasty, he was entrusted by the Qing Emperor Shunzhi with the astronomical bureau, where he continued to serve as a calendar compiler. With advanced Western astronomical knowledge, Adam Schall played an important role in modernizing Chinese astronomy.

▶ After seizing the island of Java in 1626, Dutch troops advanced to Penghu, an area under Ming jurisdiction at the time. Defeated by Ming garrison troops, the Dutch shifted their objective and occupied Taiwan Island. Under Dutch occupation, local residents were compelled to pay high taxes and sell raw silk, sugar and porcelain at low prices to the authorities, who obtained excessively high profits by reselling the goods to countries around the world. In 1662, Zheng Chenggong expelled the Dutch from Taiwan.

▶ Chen Hongshou (1598-1652), best known for his fine-brush figure paintings, was a versatile Ming artist who was accomplished in landscape, flower-and-bird, bamboo-and-rock, and other subjects. Human figures in Chen's early works were of fine form, with the clothing clearly and smoothly trimmed with ink lines; while in his late years, he would portray individuals in an exaggerated and unusual way to reveal their personalities. Also noted for painting illustrations for literary works, Chen was endowed with the ability to reveal the disposition of characters as envisioned through the literature. His extant works of woodcut prints include *Lotus and Mandarin Ducks*, *Sheng'an with Flowers on Head*, and *Nine Songs*.

Sheng'an with Flowers on Head (detail)

1629   1636

The revolt of Li Zicheng (1629-1644)

Huangtaiji, first Qing emperor

Born a peasant, Li Zicheng (1606-1645) self-proclaimed in 1629 as the "Daring King," led a rebellion against the Ming Dynasty. Under the popular slogan "equal distribution of land without taxation," Li gathered more than one million peasant soldiers. In 1644, he established the Dashun regime and captured the Ming capital Beijing the same year. Before the new regime could be consolidated, Wu Sangui, a Ming general garrisoned at the Great Wall's Shanhai Pass, opened the gates to let the Manchu into China proper. The Manchu troops expelled Li from Beijing, and drove him to Hubei Province, where he was killed by troops that were loyal to the late Ming.

Huangtaiji (1592-1643) was the eighth son of Nurhachi. As a brilliant politician and military strategist, nine years after accession he unified northeastern China. In 1636, he changed the dynasty title from "Later Jin" to "Qing," and the clan name to "Manchu." The political structure of the Qing Dynasty followed the Ming administrative system, with

Huangtaiji

imperial power strengthened through an absolute sovereign. Favorable policies were enacted to stabilize the country and develop agriculture. Essential Chinese classics and literature were maintained and integrated into the new Manchu culture. And the imperial examination system was resumed as a civil-service test to select officials for the court. The "Eight Banners" military system continued, with the Banners of Plain Yellow, Bordered Yellow, and Plain Blue under direct command of the Emperor. Two new sets of Eight Banners were also created to include Mongolian and Han sections. Although Huangtaiji failed to breach the Great Wall to bring down the Ming Dynasty, he undoubtedly laid a solid foundation for the complete victory of the Manchu.

A Ming Ministry of War report on the activities of Li Zicheng

1637　　　　　　　　　　1639

Song Yingxing and *Exploitation of the Works of Nature*

Xu Guangqi and *Complete Book of Agriculture*

Facsimile of *Exploitation of the Works of Nature*

Published in 1637, *Exploitation of the Works of Nature* (*Tiangong Kaiwu*) is regarded as the encyclopedia on technology of 17th century China. Composed of three volumes, the book covered a wide range of technical issues, introducing current technology in various industries. The issues touched upon included irrigation, hydraulic engineering, textile technology, milling processes, ceramics industry, ships and carts, iron metallurgy, mining, and other areas. Featuring detailed illustrations, the book is acknowledged as a classic on agriculture and technological subjects.

The author Song Yingxing (1587-1661), a learned local Ming official, compiled this book by utilizing his profound knowledge of technological issues and other fields.

Facsimile of *Exploitation of the Works of Nature*

Portrait of Xu Guangqi

Xu Guangqi (1562-1633), an imperial councilor of the late Ming Dynasty, devoted himself to agricultural research, and composed *Nongzheng Quanshu* (*Complete Book of Agriculture*), which was published in 1639 after his death. With some 700,000 characters in 60 volumes, the well-illustrated book discussed agricultural issues in the late Ming and reviewed Chinese agricultural history up to then. Agricultural topics covered were: field systems, agricultural tasks, water control, agricultural implements, horticulture, sericulture, textile crops, silviculture, animal husbandry, famine control, and a list of edible plants. In an agricultural society, the publication of such a book meant more than the mere summary of agricultural issues, it also served as inspiration for state affairs administration of the government.

1640-1688: The English Bourgeois Revolution.

1644 - 1911

▶ Qing Dynasty

▶ Established as Later Jin by the Manchu (descendants of the Jurchen) in 1616 and renamed Qing in 1636, the Qing Dynasty was the last feudal regime in Chinese history. From the time it entered central China and started to rule from Beijing in 1644, the Manchu dynasty lasted 268 years with 10 emperors. Its early rulers were open-minded and accomplished in political, economic and civil affairs, enabling the nation to enjoy the world's fastest-growing economy with the largest territory. However, in its later years, the Qing began to fall prey to the colonialism of Britain, France, and other industrialized Western countries. During the period of feudal-colonial society, visionary patriots started endeavors to seek a way out. One such example was the Westernization Movement, to "subdue the West by learning from them." Other responses ranged from self-improvement methods by adopting "a Westernized Chinese style," to radical revolutionary movements such as the "Hundred Days' Reform" in 1898. Finally, the Qing Dynasty was overthrown in the 1911 Revolution.

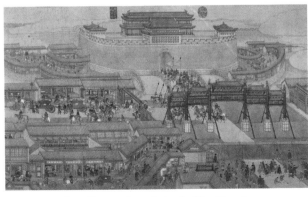

Busy Qianmen Street during the Qing Dynasty

Hairstyle decree

After establishing its regime in Beijing, the Qing government decreed in 1644 and again in 1645 that all Han Chinese men had to adopt the Manchu hairstyle, shaving the front of their heads and braiding the remaining hair into a queue behind. This was considered an act of ideological submission through physical means, and was brutally carried out. It was a capital offense if any Han man did not shave his head within 10 days of the Manchu army's arrival in the city.

Huang Zongxi and *Waiting for the Dawn*   ## Gu Yanwu

Huang Zongxi (1610-1695) was a political theorist, philosopher and soldier during the late

Huang Zongxi and a facsimile of his *Waiting for the Dawn*

Ming period. A patriot, he campaigned against the powerful eunuchs and corrupt high officials in the late Ming, and assembled volunteers to fight against the Manchu southward advance. In his *Waiting for the Dawn* (*Mingyi Daifanglu*), he openly criticized the self-serving autocratic rule, advocating that the ruler had a public responsibility toward the country. He further argued that the emperor was endangering the well-being of the nation for his own pleasure, thus a poison for the country and cause for the turbulence. To find a solution, Huang stressed the need for constitutional law, by which autocracy would turn into public governance, restricting the ruler's power. Huang's ideology inspired democratic thinking in modern China.

From the late Ming Dynasty into the early Qing, Chinese intellectuals became increasingly aware of the impracticality of the Song and Ming metaphysical theories, so they turned to more pragmatic means to bolster the national economy and improve people's livelihood. Among them, the philosopher Gu Yanwu (1613-1682) acted as a pioneer. Gu spent his youth in anti-Manchu activity, and never served the Qing Dynasty after the Ming was overthrown. Instead, he traveled throughout the country, devoting himself to historical and folklore study. As a scholar, he made great contributions to Chinese history, phonology, geography, and frontier defense. As a patriot, Gu is remembered for his saying, "Every individual has a share of responsibility towards the country."

Gu Yanwu

● Wang Fuzhi

● Emperor Kangxi (r. 1661-1722)

Wang Fuzhi

● Wang Fuzhi (1619-1692), a native of Hengyang, Hunan Province, was also known as Master Chuanshan. After the downfall of the Ming Dynasty, Wang participated in various struggles against the Manchu regime. Meeting with failure, he retired to a reclusive life in the mountains, spending the next 40 years studying and writing. He was accomplished in philosophy, history, literature, astronomy, calendric system, mathematics and geography. Strongly opposed to the Song and Ming rationalist metaphysics, Wang believed that human nature developed through practice in life, rejecting the assertion of an unchanging human nature.

● Acknowledged as a success among the Qing emperors, Emperor Kangxi (1654-1722) ascended the throne at age 7, and exercised full power by the age of 13. With the dual aim of developing the economy and easing domestic tensions, he imposed a permanent ban on land enclosure, encouraged population growth, and ordered that taxation never be increased. In 1673, he ordered the nullification of the Three Feudatories, and later crushed their rebellion. Ten years later, Shi Lang reclaimed Taiwan under Imperial Edict. After a series of battles against the Russian Empire from 1685 to 1689, Qing troops gained the advantage, and the two parties signed a peace treaty, determining the eastern border. Between 1690 and 1697, Emperor Kangxi, as commander-in-chief, launched three campaigns against the revolting Jungars,

Emperor Kangxi

Emperor Kangxi's Cruise to the South (detail)

crushing the rebellions. He also sent troops to Tibet to defend the western border. Deemed as a grand phase in Chinese history, the 61-year reign of Emperor Kangxi brought remarkable advances to the empire's economy, culture and military.

○ Mid-17th century: British scientist Robert Boyle (1627-1691), regarded as the founder of modern chemistry, introduced scientific procedures to chemistry experiments.

1662

Zhu Da

Zheng Chenggong resumed control over Taiwan

Living in the early Qing Dynasty, Zhu Da (1626-1705), also known as Badashanren (literally, "Eight-Great-Mountain Man"), was an artist of Ming royal lineage. He painted flowers-and-birds, fish-and-insects representations in an exaggerated way, leaving more white than black in animals' eyes. This peculiar way of painting was supposed to reflect the author's grief at the downfall of his country, as well as his aloofness from real conditions. The innovative style of Zhu's painting left an enduring impact on later artists, and is best represented by the works *Peony and Peacock*, *Inked Flowers*, *Flowers upon a River*, among others.

Dutch colonists in Taiwan surrendering to Zheng Chenggong

Zheng Chenggong (Koxinga) was a native of Nan'an, Fujian Province. After the Manchu took control over northern China, he rose to fight against the Qing Dynasty. With a powerful fleet at sea, he maintained control of the southeastern provinces of Fujian, Guangdong and Zhejiang for over 20 years, once even advancing into the Yangtze River regions. It was not until 1660 that the Qing armies turned the tide and forced Zheng to Xiamen. In 1662, Zheng Chenggong retreated to Dutch-occupied Taiwan with some 20,000 soldiers on several hundred ships. After first capturing Zeelandia (present-day Tainan), Zheng's troops advanced to besiege "Taiwan City" (now Anping). Zheng also defeated the Dutch reinforcements, and established a new regime in Taiwan. In 1683, Emperor Kangxi of Qing resumed authority over Taiwan, and made it a formal prefecture of China.

Flowers upon a River (detail)

Pu Songling's *Strange Tales from Make-do Studio*

Shi Tao

Establishment of Taiwan Prefecture

Pu Songling (1640-1715) was an impoverished writer who lived during the Qing Dynasty. He spent his lifetime collecting folklore and anecdotes, compiling *Strange Tales from Make-do Studio* in 1679. Composed of 491 short stories, the book recounts supernatural tales of humans and various creatures such as vixen spirits, gods, ghosts, beasts, and demons. With captivating description, the strange tales reflect the author's disillusionment with society, exposing the corrupt government, defects in the imperial examination system and the decadent social system.

A Clear Autumn Day in Yangzhou (detail)

Shi Tao (1642-1718), with the original family name Zhu and religious name Yuanji, was a Qing artist of Ming royal lineage. Absorbing the essence of previous master brushworks, he developed his own landscape style through innovation and observation of nature. Shi Tao believed in "learning from previous masters to create new styles" and "learning from nature to inspire new works." His masterpieces include *Collection of Astonishing Mountains* and *A Clear Autumn Day in Yangzhou*.

In 1684, the Qing Dynasty formally established Taiwan Prefecture, placing it under the Jurisdiction of Fujian Province. The prefecture governed the counties of Taiwan, Fengshan and Zhuluo. On October 12, 1885, the Qing government promoted Taiwan to a province, naming Liu Mingchuan as its governor.

An imperial inspector's tour in Taiwan during the reign of Qing Emperor Yongzheng

A Qing Dynasty illustrated copy of *Strange Tales from Make-do Studio*

○ 1687: English scientist Isaac Newton (1642-1727) published *Philosophiæ Naturalis Principia Mathematica* (*Mathematical Principles of Natural Philosophy*), marking the foundation of Classical Mechanics.

○ 1688: The Glorious Revolution in England.

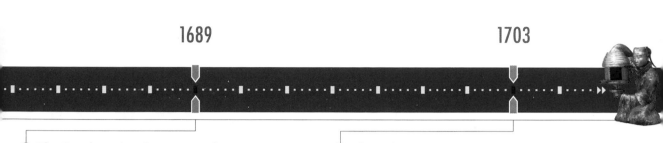

1689

1703

The Russian-Manchu Treaty of Nibuchu (Nerchinsk)

Chengde Summer Resort (1703-1792)

Chengde Summer Resort

From the late 16th century onwards, Russia constantly plagued the northeastern regions of China, but was defeated each time by Chinese garrison troops. In 1689, the first peace treaty between the two countries was signed at the border town of Nibuchu (Nerchinsk). According to the treaty, the eastern border between the two countries became set along the Ergun and Gerbici rivers, extending along the Outer Hinggan Mountains to the sea. China controlled the lands south of the border, while Russia had those to the north. People with travel documents were allowed to cross the border, and border trade was also permitted.

Located 100 km north of Beijing, Chengde is a natural summer resort surrounded by mountain ranges. In 1703, Emperor Kangxi ordered the construction of an imperial palace as a summer resort in Chengde. The construction lasted 90 years, presenting a grand palace complex upon its completion: with a total area of 5,640,000 sq m, and over 110 sites in the palace and scenery-viewing sections. Manchu emperors resided at the Chengde resort every summer to avoid the sultry weather in Beijing, and the early emperors of Qing would even spend half the year here.

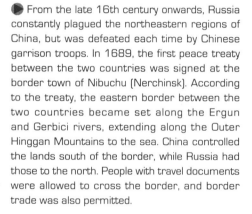

○ 1689: England's Parliament passed the "Bill of Rights," marking the establishment of a constitutional monarchy in Britain.

○ 1690: English empiricist John Locke (1632-1704) published *An Essay Concerning Human Understanding*, detailing the idea of constitutional government.

173

1713

1723

The imperial conferral of the Dalai and Panchen Lamas

Emperor Yongzheng (r. 1723-1735)

In 1653, Emperor Shunzhi of Qing bestowed the title of "Dalai Lama" on the 5th Dalai. "Dalai" means "sea" in Mongolian, while "Lama" is "great teacher" in Tibetan. In 1713, Emperor Kangxi delegated an imperial envoy to recognize the 5th Panchen as the "Panchen Erdeni." "Panchen"

The fifth Dalai Lama meeting with Emperor Shunzhi

means "great scholar" in Sanskrit; "Erdeni" is "treasure" in Manchu. Through imperial conferral of the Dalai and Panchen Lamas, the Qing Dynasty hereafter established the system of central sanction of the religious leaders of Tibet. This system carried forward the relationship between the central government and Tibet from the Yuan and Ming dynasties, and is still in use today.

The imperial edict of Emperor Kangxi recognizing the fifth Panchen Erdeni

As the third Manchu emperor to rule over China proper, Emperor Yongzheng reigned for a brief period of 13 years, during which the Qing further bloomed into full prosperity under his innovative and diligent governance. A remarkable tax reform took place in 1724, when Emperor Yongzheng ordered that the poll tax be replaced by taxation according to area of land owned. This policy abolished the obligatory poll tax, which had existed in China for thousands of years. From 1726 to 1731, he carried out political reforms in southwestern China, where diverse nationalities resided, changing the hereditary system of administration by local chieftains to appointment of local administrators by the central government. In 1729, he set up the Military Council, with his power further centralized. This series of policies laid a solid foundation for the grand Qianlong era that followed.

Emperor Yongzheng Conducting a Ritual Ceremony at the Altar of the God of Agriculture (detail)

Complete Literature from Earliest to Current Times

Emperor Qianlong (r. 1736-1795)

Compiled by Chen Menglei during the region of Emperor Kangxi, the compilation of the encyclopedic work *Gujin Tushu Jicheng [Complete Literature from Earliest to Current Times]* started in 1700, with the first draft completed six years later. Containing a complete portfolio of literature from remote times to the 18th century, the book was given its title by Emperor Kangxi. During the Yongzheng period, Jiang Tingxi further edited and polished the book. The revised version was completed and published in 1728. Famed as the "Qing Encyclopedia," it was divided into six sections, containing 10,000 chapters in 5,000 volumes, totaling 144 million Chinese characters.

Emperor Qianlong Inspecting Armies (detail)

Emperor Yongzheng's fourth son, Emperor Qianlong (1711-1795) reigned for 60 years, pushing the Qing Dynasty to its zenith. During his reign, he crushed rebellions of local forces in northwest China, tightened control of the areas on both sides of the Tianshan Mountains, and issued the Regulations of Imperial Jurisdiction over Tibet, thus strengthening the central government's authority over Tibet to maintain the integrity of Chinese territory. However, due to conceit, he spent huge sums of money to display his greatness and success. Heshen, the most corrupt official in Chinese history, was his favorite official.

Heshen

Heshen (1750-1799) was the favorite official of Emperor Qianlong. He served as Qianlong's military minister for 24 years while holding many other crucial posts. In the latter phase of the Qianlong era, Heshen enjoyed overwhelming power in the court, openly and widely abusing his power, leading to decline of national power and widespread corruption among officials. After the death of Emperor Qianlong, the newly ascended Emperor Jiaqing immediately prosecuted Heshen for 20 capital offenses, and ordered him to commit suicide. His confiscated property counted in billions of taels of silver.

Portrait of Heshen

● Zheng Banqiao

● Publication of *Twenty-Four Histories* (1739-1784)

Bamboo and Rock, by Zheng Banqiao

● The Qing artist Zheng Xie (1693-1765), styled Banqiao, was noted for his accomplishments in poetry, calligraphy and painting. An expert at painting orchid and bamboo, Zheng utilized sidestroke brushwork to vitalize the elegance and vigor of his subject matter. As for poetry, he often wrote in natural language to express sympathy for a suffering people as well as his disillusionment with the government. As a calligrapher, he developed a unique style between the running script and the official script, and introduced a painting approach to present an unruly spirit between the lines.

Facsimiles of *Twenty-Four Histories*

● In ancient China, it was a tradition for new regimes to revise the historical texts of the preceding dynasty. During Emperor Qianlong's reign, upon the completion of *History of Ming* in 1739, he ordered the reprinting of official histories of previous dynasties. Completed in 1784, they amounted to 24 titles, collectively known as *Twenty-Four Histories*. They were: *Records of the Historian, Book of Han, Book of Later Han, Records of the Three Kingdoms, Book of Jin, Book of Song, Book of Southern Qi, Book of Liang, Book of Chen, Book of Wei, Book of Northern Qi, Book of Zhou, Book of Sui, History of Southern Dynasties, History of Northern Dynasties, Book of Tang, New Book of Tang, Five Dynasties History, New History of the Five Dynasties, History of Song, History of Liao, History of Jin, History of Yuan,* and *History of Ming.*

▶ Wu Jingzi and *The Scholars*

▶ Dai Zhen

▶ Guangzhou, the official foreign trade port

Facsimile of
The Scholars

▶ Born into an aristocratic family, the Qing writer Wu Jingzi (1701-1754) suffered many setbacks in his pursuit of an official career. As his life fell into poverty, Wu composed a novel to tell the tragic fate of unsuccessful literati trapped in the imperial examination system of his time. In this novel, Wu fleshed out the characters of unfortunate scholars, victims of court corruption and a decaying examination system. The novel's bitter true-to-life descriptions made *The Scholars* a representative work of Chinese literary realism and satire.

▶ Dai Zhen (1723-1777) was a Qing philosopher and textual researcher. He opposed the metaphysical approach to exploring the world. Instead, he believed truth was to be revealed only through careful observation and analysis. Dai condemned rationalist ideas as "killing people for principle," arguing it was even crueler than "killing people by law." A logical scholar, Dai attached great importance to meticulous textual research of data. He was noted for his phonological research and critical interpretation of ancient texts, and recognized as an exemplary figure in Qing practical scholarship.

▶ In 1757, Emperor Qianlong constricted foreign trade at China's coastal ports, authorizing Guangzhou as the only trade port. In addition, foreign traders could do business only with official trade companies, and had to stay in specified locations. Guangzhou thus became the only official trade port of China during the period from the mid-18th century to the mid-19th century. The reason why Emperor Qianlong enacted such a policy was partially attributed to his self-imposed conceit, but it was also a precautionary measure against foreign adventurers and smugglers.

The Port of Guangzhou in the 18th century

◎ 1748: French philosopher Charles de Montesquieu (1689-1755) published *De l'esprit des lois* (*The Spirit of the Laws*), proposing the separation of legislative, judicial and executive powers.

◎ French philosopher and writer Voltaire (1694-1778), an important figure in the French Enlightenment.

◎ 1762: *Du Contrat Social* (*The Social Contract*) by French philosopher Jean-Jacques Rousseau (1712-1778) was published.

Cao Xueqin and *A Dream of Red Mansions*

Cao Xueqin (1724-1764) was a member of an early 18th century aristocratic family, who led extravagant lives until the clan's decline. While living in poverty in his old age, Cao composed *A Dream of Red Mansions* to mirror his own life. The lengthy masterpiece tells of the fortunes and misfortunes of an aristocratic family in the 18th century, following the main theme of the tragic romance of the main characters Jia Baoyu, Lin Daiyu and Xue Baochai. Acknowledged as a remarkable apex in Chinese literaty classics, the novel even gave birth to a new academic discipline — "Hongxue" or research on *Red Mansions*.

Portrait of characters from
A Dream of Red Mansions

Siku Quanshu (*Complete Library in the Four Branches of Literature*) (1772-1782)

Facsimiles of *Complete Library in the Four Branches of Literature*

In 1772, over 3,800 scholars were summoned under the imperial edict of Emperor Qianlong to compile *Siku Quanshu* (*Complete Library in the Four Branches of Literature*). Upon completion of the grand project 10 years later, the collection included more than 36,000 books from the contemporary and previous historical periods and dynasties, and became known as the most complete encyclopedia of Chinese culture. During the process of compilation, Emperor Qianlong ordered all anti-Manchu writings destroyed. *Siku Quanshu* had eight copies, which were stored in different places in the country, but only three and a half have survived the past 200 years of chaotic times.

○ 1776: British scholar and economist Adam Smith (1723-1790) published *The Wealth of Nations*, which brought him the fame as "father of modern economics."

○ 1776: At the 2nd Continental Congress, 13 British North American colonies jointly issued the "Declaration of Independence," proclaiming the foundation of the United States of America, with George Washington (1732-1799) as commander in chief. In 1783, the defeated English government acknowledged the independence of the US.

○ German philosopher Immanuel Kant (1724-1804) published a series of works summarizing the Enlightenment: *Critique of Pure Reason, Critique of Practical Reason*, and *Critique of Judgment*.

Literary Purges

Beijing Opera

The early Qing emperors were very sensitive to anti-Manchu sentiments among the Han Chinese people. Intellectuals who wrote about the Ming Dynasty would be killed; and certain words written, such as "Qing, Ming, Yi (barbarian)," could also lead to the death penalty. During the 130 years of emperors Kangxi, Yongzheng and Qianlong, more than 70 literary purges were carried out, and a great number of people were killed. One purpose of Emperor Qianlong's compilation of *Complete Library in the Four Branches of Literature* was to censor all the books in the country, banning and destroying those suspicious of anti-Manchu sentiment.

In 1790, four famous Anhui Opera troupes came to Beijing to celebrate the 80th birthday of Emperor Qianlong, and a new genre of performance was born through half-a-century's merging of the characteristics of Anhui Opera and other theatrical types. The new genre was named "Beijing Opera," which gradually became a national treasure of stage. As a form of traditional Chinese theater, Beijing Opera combines the skills of singing, monologue, acting, combat and dancing to tell stories and describe characters. Generally there are five roles in Beijing Opera: *Sheng* (male), *Dan* (female), *Jing* (painted face male), *Mo* (old male), and *Chou* (clown), differentiated by the costumes or colors of masks. The singing styles mainly feature *Xipi* and *Erhuang* melodies, to the accompaniment of traditional musical instruments such as the *jinghu*, *erhu*, *yueqin*, and percussion instruments.

19th century opera performance in a teahouse

1780s: The steam engine, invented and improved by James Watt, was put to use, marking the beginning of the Age of Steam.

1787: The US Constitution was adopted as a federal constitution, stipulating the separation of the three powers and the principle of a federal, democratic and republican country. The US Constitution is acknowledged as the first complete written bourgeois constitution.

▶ Ji Xiaolan

▶ Reincarnation system established to identify Dalai and Panchen Lamas

▶ The Qing Imperial Grand Councilor Ji Xiaolan (1724-1805) was a witty personage noted in the court for his profound knowledge and exquisite essays. Ji led several imperial publication projects, the most famous being *Complete Library in the Four Branches of Literature*, during the Qianlong Region. He personally wrote a 200-volume catalogue for the *Complete Library*.

▶ To seek the reincarnated child of the "living Buddha" in Tibetan Buddhism, a system of utilizing a golden urn was set in 1793 by the Qing emperor. In the edict "29 Regulations on Tibetan Affairs," Emperor Qianlong made specific regulations on Tibetan religion, administration, finance, military, and foreign relations. The reincarnation system was listed first in the document. When the preceding Dalai or Panchen Lamas passed away, the most eminent high monks would begin searching for reincarnated children. If more than one reincarnation was found, the children would be raised and educated at the same time. When they reached the age of six, their names would be written on jade lots and put into a gold urn to be drawn. Once the reincarnation was decided, an enthronement ceremony would be held to recognize him as the next Dalai or Panchen Lama.

A gold urn and jade lots used in reincarnation rituals in the Qing Dynasty

Ji Xiaolan

© 1789-1794: During the French Revolution, the *Declaration of the Rights of Man* was announced at the National Assembly.

© 1804: Napoleon Bonaparte (1769-1821), self-proclaimed Emperor of France, replaced the First French Republic with the "First French Empire."

Macartney Embassy to China   Gong Zizhen   Cheng Changgeng

In July 1793, appointed by George III of Britain as an envoy, George Macartney led the first British embassy to China, with the hope of setting up a permanent British embassy in Beijing. At the imperial court, Emperor Qianlong insisted that Macartney must follow the ritual of kowtowing to show respect. However, Macartney proposed that he would kowtow only if a Chinese official equal to his status would kowtow to an image of George III. The argument ended in Macartney's refusal to perform the ritual.

The Macartney Embassy meeting Emperor Qianlong

The Qing philosopher Gong Zizhen (1792-1841) proposed studying practical knowledge for application in solving political and social problems. Gong himself concentrated on studies of legal institution and geographical features of border areas, reminding the emperor of the importance of guarding against possible foreign invasions. In his literary works, Gong broke the tradition from the mid-Qing Dynasty of only describing natural scenery, by extending his comments to current policies and social problems.

Cheng Changgeng in theatrical costume

A native of Anhui, Cheng Changgeng (1811-1880) joined an Anhui Opera troupe as an apprentice at a young age. In 1822, he followed his father to Beijing, making his mark on theater with *Wenzhaoguan* and *Battle in Changsha*. Integrating the characteristics of Anhui, Kunqu and Hubei operas, Cheng's vocal performance featured vigorous high-pitch singing with clear pronunciation. In stage performance, the social status, personality and inner feelings of the characters were well revealed through Cheng's mature stage style. For his contributions to theater, Cheng is regarded as the master of Anhui Opera as well as the founder of Beijing Opera.

1810-1826: Independence movement in Spanish Latin America.

1814: The political map of Europe was reset at the Congress of Vienna.

1823: US President James Monroe (1758-1831) issued the "Monroe Doctrine" to prevent Europe from interfering with the independence of European colonies in the Americas.

Lin Zexu's campaign to
suppress opium

The First Opium War (1840-1842)

Lin Zexu

In late 1838, Lin Zexu (1785-1850) was sent to Guangdong as imperial commissioner to halt the illegal import of opium by the English. Lin fortified coastal defense, recruited militia, arrested and punished opium dealers and corrupt officials, and confiscated 1,200 tons of opium from English and US traders. In June 1839, Lin ordered the destruction of opium in Humen town, and drove off multiple subsequent English invasions. Lin's suppression of opium was a signal of the resolve of Chinese people against the poison.

Battle scene between China and Britain at
Guangzhou during the First Opium War

China's resistance to opium was disastrous to England's profits in China and Asia. Frustrated, the English government sent naval forces to attack China's coastlines, and forced the latter into negotiation. However, during the negotiation, English armies occupied Hong Kong and Humen, attacked Guangzhou and other ports along the coastal provinces of Fujian, Zhejiang and Jiangsu. With no agreement reached, the English further occupied Xiamen and Shanghai, threatening Nanjing along the Yangtze River. The First Opium War lasted over two years, and ended with China ceding territory and paying reparations to Britain.

◎ 1831: English scientist Michael Faraday (1791-1867) discovered electromagnetic induction.

◎ 1830s-1840s: Three major labour movements in Europe: Canut revolts in Lyon, France; Chartism in Britain; and textile workers' uprising in Silesia, Germany.

Treaty of Nanjing ● **Wei Yuan and *Illustrated Treatise on the Maritime Kingdoms***

● With Nanjing threatened by English troops, the Qing government was forced to sign the Treaty of Nanjing in 1842, the first unequal treaty in Chinese history. The treaty included the following terms: first, the payment of a large sum in reparations; second, the ceding of Hong Kong; and third, the opening of Guangzhou, Xiamen, Fuzhou, Ningbo and Shanghai as trade ports with negotiated tariffs. Coveting the great profits England enjoyed, the USA, France, Spain, Italy and other industrialized countries swarmed in to claim the same privileges stipulated in the treaty. China was rendered to a semi-colonial status.

Facsimile of
*Illustrated Treatise
on the Maritime
Kingdoms*

● A contemporary of Gong Zizhen, Qing philosopher Wei Yuan (1794-1857) once held an official post, but resigned due to his dissatisfaction with the emperor's lack of resolve. He advocated the application of academic studies to social issues and the reform of old practices. With his 1842 *Illustrated Treatise on the Maritime Kingdoms* [*Hai Guo Tu Zhi*], Wei became the first scholar to introduce European history, geography, politics, economy and culture to China. To encourage the introduction of European science and technology, he proposed, "Learning the advantages from the West in order to subdue them." For his broadmindedness, Wei is considered one of the heralds of learning from the West in modern Chinese history.

Hong Kong opened trade with foreign countries

○ French realist writer Honoré de Balzac (1799-1850) wrote a sequence of novels and plays collectively entitled *La Comédie Humaine*, including *Eugénie Grandet* and *Le Père Goriot*.

○ French romanticist writer Victor Hugo (1802-1885) wrote *Notre Dame de Paris*, *The Miserable*, and *Ninety-Three*, among other novels.

○ 1840: Upon the completion of the Industrial Revolution, England became the first industrialized country in the world.

Shanghai International Settlement

The Taiping Heavenly Kingdom (1851-1864)

In November 1845, George Balfour, the first English consul in Shanghai, forced local officials to encircle the area north of Yangjingbang Creek and south of Lijiachang, as an English settlement district. In 1863, the USA encircled large areas of land north of the Suzhou River as a US concession. Later that year, the English and US foreign concessions were combined as the "Shanghai International Settlement," the earliest foreign settlement in China. The district was wholly foreign controlled and administered, as a "nation within a nation."

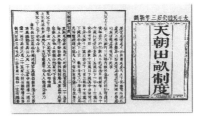

The Land System of the Heavenly Kingdom, guiding platform of the Taiping Kingdom

Hong Xiuquan

A large-scale peasant revolt in south China broke out amidst Western threats to the Qing government. Hong Xiuquan (1814-1864), the leader of the rebellion, had failed to pass the imperial exam several times. In 1851, he declared the uprising of the "Taiping (Great Peace) Heavenly Kingdom" in Jintian Village in Guangxi's Guiping County. In fact, Hong had set up Baishangdihui (Worshipers of God) in 1843, as a secret sect, where he preached Christianity in relation to peasants' interests, convincing them to join the revolt. In 1853, their forces captured Nanjing, renamed as "Tianjing," becoming their "Heavenly Capital." Over the following 11 years, most of south China came under the control of the Taiping Kingdom, with even Beijing threatened for a time. The Qing government was forced to authorize local officials to organize armies, while seeking help from Western powers. The movement was not put down until 1864.

Shanghai International Settlement

© English writer Charles Dickens (1812-1870) wrote *David Copperfield*, *Bleak House*, *Hard Times*, *Great Expectations*, *A Tale of Two Cities*, and other novels.

● Rong Hong

● The Second Opium War (1856-1860)

Rong Hong

● In 1847, the 18-year-old Rong Hong (1828-1912) left his hometown in Xiangshan, Guangdong Province, with his foreign teacher for the US. Seven years later, Rong graduated with honors from Yale University, as the first Chinese student ever to graduate from a US university. He returned to China in 1855, proposing to the Qing government that children aged 12 to 15 be selected nationwide to study in the US. In 1872, as a supervisor he led 30 students to the US, and was appointed as China's vice-consul in the US. In 1876, Rong received a doctorate degree in law with high honors from Yale University.

The Second Opium War

● Beginning in 1854, Western powers demanded free trade throughout China and the legalization of the opium trade. Their demands rejected, English troops attacked Guangzhou in 1856. Later the Anglo-French allied forces advanced north along the coast with the support of Russia and the US. They attacked Tianjin and occupied Beijing, where they burnt down the Old Summer Palace after looting it. The Second Opium War ended with a series of unequal treaties signed between the Qing government and the Western allied powers.

During the Second Opium War, the Qing government signed a series of unequal treaties with the Western allied powers, including the 1858 Treaties of Tianjin, with England, France, the USA and Russia; 1858 Treaty of Aigun, with Russia; and 1860 Convention of Peking, with England, France and Russia. According to these treaties, China was forced to pay a large sum of war indemnities, further open ports in the Yangtze River region, allow permanent foreign embassies in Beijing, and allow foreign missionaries to proselytize freely in China. Apart from the indemnity, Russia gained more than 1,000,000 sq km of land in northeast China.

◎ 1854: The Crimean War broke out as a result of Russian-French disputes over their interests in the Ottoman Empire.

1859   1860

Hong Renxuan and *A New Book on Administration*

Burning of the Old Summer Palace

Facsimile of *A New Book on Administration*

Hong Renxuan (1822-1864) was a leader of the Taiping Kingdom in its later years. Once a sojourner in Hong Kong, Hong took over the administration of the Kingdom in 1860. In the same year, he wrote *Zizheng Xinpian* (*A New Book on Administration*), proposing a set of innovative policies to learn capitalism from the West. Hong's ideas were never realized, the regime being seriously endangered due to internal and external factors. The Taiping Movement was put down in 1864, with Hong captured and killed.

The main contents of Hong's book were:
1. centralization of power, prohibition of cliques, and encouragement of the free airing of views;
2. learning from Western capitalism to develop industry and mining, communications, postal services, finance, and irrigation systems;
3. encouraging private industries and inventions;
4. free and equal trade and intercourse between China and foreign countries, to learn advanced technologies;
5. establishment of banks and issuing of banknotes;
6. discarding retrograde customs, while building schools, hospitals, and welfare organizations.

Ruins of Yuanmingyuan (Old Summer Palace)

Situated in the suburbs of Beijing, Yuanmingyuan (Old Summer Palace) was built in the 18th century, covering an area of 350 ha. The grand imperial garden was a masterpiece in Chinese garden architecture. With numerous treasures, classics and antiques, the garden was hailed as the "Garden of Gardens." On 11 October 1860, the Anglo-French coalition occupied Beijing, and attacked the Yuanmingyuan over seven days. They looted all that could be carried away, smashed what could not, and set fire to the palace on October 18 under the British commander Elgin. The fire lasted for three days, burning the grand palace to the ground, killing 300 eunuchs, maids and gardeners.

© 1859: Charles Darwin (1809-1882) published *On the Origin of Species*, proposing the theory of natural selection.

The "treaty system"

Empress Dowager Cixi's reign behind the curtain (1861-1908)

Current Situation, a satirical cartoon in the late Qing

The "treaty system" referred to the Western control over China in the 1840s through signed treaties accompanied by military threats. Large areas of China's territories were ceded, foreign settlements were set up in Chinese cities, China's export trade and exchange were controlled, and extraterritoriality was granted to foreigners. In this way, China's economy entered the world market to the benefit of foreign powers, as an enslaved China struggled on its modernization path.

When Emperor Xianfeng died of illness in 1861, his successor, Emperor Tongzhi, ascended the throne at only age five, leaving real power in the hands of his mother, Empress Dowager Cixi. Over the following 47 years, Cixi actually reigned behind the curtain. Under her leadership, China saw a brief period of development. However, her desire for power led to the persecution of officials with different views domestically, and the undermining of national strength by the signing of humiliating treaties with Western powers. When she died, the once powerful Qing Dynasty was on the brink of collapse.

Empress Dowager Cixi

Westernization Movement (1861-1895)
Zongli Yamen (Office for Affairs of All Nations)

Yixin, Prince Gong

 Initiated by a pragmatic faction in the Qing court, the "Westernization Movement" aimed to improve the national power of China, but without any changes in the political structure. The movement's leadership included Prince Gong (1832-1898), the younger brother of Emperor Xianfeng, and the progressive officials Zeng Guofan, Zuo Zongtang, Li Hongzhang, and Zhang Zhidong. A set of plans was proposed and put into practice: military Westernization by purchasing foreign guns and gunboats to equip modern armies and building up arsenals and shipyards; economic reforms by setting up civil industries in mining and communications; educational modernization by opening new schools to teach European languages and sciences, as well as sending students to study in the West. The Movement lasted over 30 years, until the end of the 19th century.

 In 1861, the Office for Affairs of All Nations was established to deal with increasing foreign exchanges due to the opening of new trade ports and entry of foreign consuls to Beijing. The Zongli Yamen was a central office in charge of foreign affairs, trade affairs, arms trade, and education (building new schools and sending students overseas). The staff was composed of progressive Chinese and some foreigners, with prominent foreign figures as counselors. In 1901, the name of the office was changed to the "Office of Foreign Affairs."

Office for Affairs of All Nations

© 1860s: The start of the Second Industrial Revolution

Zeng Guofan

Li Hongzhang

Portrait of Zeng Guofan

▶ Zeng Guofan (1811-1872), a native of Xiangxiang, Hunan Province, served as a civil official in the Qing government. In 1852, to help the government suppress the Taiping Heavenly Kingdom, Zeng raised in his hometown a military force, which was later known as the "Xiang Army." His chance to capture Wuhan came when the Taiping movement became divided internally. For his military victories, Zeng was promoted as Viceroy of Liangjiang, and soon afterwards became Imperial Commissioner in charge of an army of 200,000 men. In 1864, Zeng's troops captured Tianjing, the Taiping Kingdom's capital. Over the following eight years, Zeng exerted his influence on the policymakers of the government to push the Westernization Movement.

Li Hongzhang

▶ Similar to his mentor Zeng Guofan, Li Hongzhang (1823-1901) also started his official career by organizing local troops. As a representative figure of the Westernization Movement, Li participated in various domestic affairs from the 1860s until his death 40 years later. In the military, Li was an active figure in building arsenals to produce modern war vessels and cannons. Economically, he set up a number of civil industries to reestablish China's national strength and prosperity. In education, he opened new schools and sent students to study in Western countries. He was also the initiator of the Navy Department and the Beiyang Fleet. As Minister of Foreign Affairs, Li signed a series of humiliating treaties with the Western powers, including the Treaty of Shimonoseki with Japan and the Boxer Protocol with the Eight-Nation Alliance.

China Merchants Steamship Navigation Company, established by Li Hongzhang

○ 1861: Russian Emperor Alexander II abolished serfdom, leading Russia towards becoming a capitalist country.
○ 1861-1865: The US Civil War, after which the nation was united as one.

Zhang Zhidong · School of Combined Learning · Xu Shou

Zhang Zhidong

Zhang Zhidong (1837-1909) was a native of Hebei Province. During his service as governor of Huguang, Zhang was committed to industrial development, setting up the Hanyang Iron Works, Hubei Arsenal, and bureaus of weaving, spinning, filature, and linen production. Zhang was also an educator who advocated the opening of new schools to study and teach Western technologies. His assertion was summarized in his phrase "Chinese learning for fundamental principles and Western learning for practical application."

The year 1862 saw the establishment in Beijing of Tongwen Guan, or School of Combined Learning. It was China's first new school, which adopted a classroom system to train translators and modern professionals. The school had its own press and translation office, where Western books on natural sciences, international law and economy were translated and published. Chemistry laboratories, museums and observatories were also set up in the school. The graduates of Tongwen Guan mainly served as translators or interpreters in the government, as diplomats in the Foreign Affairs Office, or officials in various modern institutions.

The site of Tongwen Guan in Beijing

Xu Shou (1818-1884) was a pioneering figure of modern chemistry in Qing-dynasty China. In 1862, he designed and produced China's first wooden steamship. Later, Xu devoted himself to the translation and propagation of Western chemistry. The works he translated and edited included: *Principles and Applications of Chemistry*, *Chemistry Inorganic and Organic with Experiments*, *List of Chemical Substances*, and *List of Western Medicine*. In 1874, Xu established the Gezhi Academy in Shanghai, a school where modern Western chemistry was taught. Xu also contributed to the naming of chemical elements.

© 1864: The International Workers Association (1st International) was founded at a London assembly attended by worker representatives from various nations.

© 1864-1870: The Prussian wars that led to the unification of Germany.

1863

Wu Changshuo

Robert Hart and China's customs (1863-1908)

Born to a scholarly family, Wu Changshuo (1844-1927) was famed for his calligraphy, painting, and seal carving. Wu's style in calligraphy was a combination of the powerful yet light use of strokes with verve and energy. His cursive hand featured the use of seal characters in a free and natural style. Wu was also reputed for his flower painting, where techniques of seal characters and cursive hand were employed in mature and vibrant depiction of plum blossoms, vines, bamboo, and chrysanthemum. With his innovative integration of poetry, calligraphy, painting, and seal carving, Wu exerted a lasting influence on modern Chinese grand freehand flower-and-bird painting.

Plum Blossoms
(detail)

Foreign staff at Chinese customs during the late Qing

In 1861, the General Customs Office was established under the Zongli Yamen to manage customs affairs with full powers over personnel, administration and finance. According to the unequal treaties, China's customs was subject to foreign control, with a foreigner as Inspector-General. Irishman Robert Hart (1835-1911) took up office as the second Inspector-General in 1863, and held the position for 45 years, participating in China's military, political, economic, diplomatic, cultural and educational affairs. During his service, Hart established a complete system in customs management, specifying strict regulations in tax collection, statistical management, dredging works, and quarantine inspection. He was also credited with setting up a modern postal service in China. However, Hart's control of Chinese customs was an infringement of Chinese sovereignty, and he served essentially to protect the trade interests of Western powers; the interests of China were thus impaired.

○ 1860s: Russian chemist Dmitri Mendeleyev (1818-1883) predicted the pattern of chemical elements and created the Periodic Table of Elements.

○ 1867: Karl Marx (1834-1907) published the first volume of *Capital*, establishing the theory of scientific socialism.

○ 1868: Upon his ascension to the throne, Emperor Meiji of Japan ended the Shogun era with the Meiji Restoration.

1872

1880

Chinese overseas students to the USA

In the summer of 1872, Rong Hong, the first overseas student in Chinese history, led 30 young students to the United States for study. For the next three years, the Qing government made a yearly selection of 30 students to study in foreign countries. The 120 students sent abroad during the four-year period were the earliest officially dispatched overseas students.

A group photo of the first Chinese overseas students

Huang Zunxian

Huang Zongxian

A native of Guangdong, Huang Zunxian (1848-1905) served for over a decade in the overseas offices of the late Qing. A revolutionary figure in modern Chinese poetry, Huang employed a realistic approach to reflect social reality, condemn autocracy, advocate reformism, and introduce Western sciences. Huang adopted the techniques of prose writing to compose lengthy dynamic poems with ancient flavor.

Establishment of China's National Telegraph Bureau

In 1880, Li Hongzhang set up the first telegraph bureau in Tianjin — formally named as the National Telegraph Bureau the next year. In 1882, the bureau was restructured into an industrial enterprise under government supervision. Later, the headquarters were moved to Shanghai to attract more investment. In 1907, the Qing government established the Post and Telegraph Administration and bought over the bureau. Four years later, the bureau was moved to Beijing and became the Post and Telegraph Administration. The establishment of the Administration marked the historical end of the post-house courier system in China, and gave birth to a modern communications system.

1870: The Third Republic of France was founded. A constitution was passed in 1875, marking the establishment of a bourgeois republic

Russian writer Leo Tolstoy (1828-1910) wrote the master works *War and Peace*, *Anna Karenina* and *Resurrection*, etc.

1871: Establishment of the German Empire under a constitutional monarchy. On March 18, the Paris Commune was founded, ruling for a brief period until its downfall at the end of May.

1883

Tan Xinpei

Sino-French War (1883-1885)

Zheng Guanying

Tan Xinpei

A native of Hubei Province, Tan Xinpei was an eminent Beijing Opera performer in the late Qing. Tan developed a unique style in the four elements of Beijing Opera: singing, monologue, acting, and combat. Tan's vocal performance featured emotive melodious intonation, while his monologue was clear with fluent utterance of lines, and his combat performance nimble and swift. As a founder of the Tan Style, he was acknowledged as "King of Beijing Opera."

In 1883, French colonists launched several assaults on Sino-Vietnamese borders. The next year, French troops attacked Qing garrison troops in Langson, and Qing naval fleets in Taiwan and Fujian. French troops suffered severe defeats during the war, resulting in the collapse of the French cabinet. The Qing government, rather than take the chance to claim victory, offered to sign the "New Sino-French Treaty." China lost an important fleet on the southeastern coasts, and gave France free access to Yunnan, Guangxi and Guangzhou.

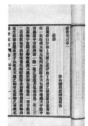

Facsimile of *Warnings to a Prosperous Age*

A native of Guangdong, Zheng Guanying (1842-1921) was a late-Qing industrialist and reformist who ran several modern industries. In his book *Shengshi Weiyan* (*Warnings to a Prosperous Age*), Zheng analyzed, from political, economic, military and cultural perspectives, the necessity for China to develop capitalist industry and commerce. He also advocated a constitutional monarchy as a new political system, and the cultivation of professionals in science and technology.

- US writer Mark Twain (1835-1910) wrote *The Gilded Age*, *The Adventures of Tom Sawyer*, *Life on the Mississippi*, *Adventures of Huckleberry Fin*, among other works.
- With over 1,000 inventions, Thomas Edison (1847-1931) pushed forward the applications of electricity.
- 1882: Establishment of the Triple Alliance between Germany, Austria-Hungary, and Italy.
- 1886: The Eight-Hour Day Strike in Chicago, as the origins of May Day.

Sun Yat-sen

Sun Yat-sen

Sun Yat-sen (1866-1925), a native of Guangdong, was a great forerunner of Chinese revolution. In 1894, Sun founded the Xingzhonghui (Revive China Society), where he gathered patriots to prepare for an uprising in Guangzhou. In 1905, Sun initiated the founding of the Tongmenghui (Chinese United League) in Tokyo, with the platform "to overthrow the Manchu empire and to restore China to the Chinese, to establish a republic, and to distribute land equally among the people." In line with the platform was the "Three Principles of the People" (nationalism, democracy, and public welfare), a political philosophy proposed by Sun. After the 1911 Chinese Revolution, Sun was elected provisional president of the Republic of China. The next year he abdicated the post to Yuan Shikai, and concentrated on the nation's economic construction. In January 1924, Sun presided over the first Kuomintang National Congress, restructured the Kuomintang (Nationalist Party), and proposed alliances with the Soviet Union (USSR) and the Communist Party, calling for support for agriculture and industry. In the same year, Sun established the Whampoa Military Academy, the most eminent military school of the time, to train military commanders for the army. Sun died of liver cancer on March 12, 1925, in Beijing.

The oath made by Sun Yat-sen at his swearing-in ceremony as the provisional president of the Republic of China

Revive China Society

Founded by Sun Yat-sen in 1894, Xingzhonghui (Revive China Society) was the first openly revolutionary organization in China. Its headquarters were located in Honolulu at its founding, and moved to Hong Kong the next year. The political platform was: "Expel foreigners, revive China, and establish a unified government." In 1905, the Chinese United League was created through the merging of the Revive China Society, Huaxinghui (China Arise Society) and Guangfuhui (Restoration Society).

Some members of the Society for the Revival of China in Japan

1889: Workers' delegations met in Paris to found the International Working Union of Socialist Parties (2nd International).

1889: Upon release of its constitution, Japan became the first constitutional state in Asia.

1895

● First Sino-Japanese War (1894-1895) **● Treaty of Shimonoseki**

Battle scene at sea during
the First Sino-Japanese War

● Following China's defeat in the first Sino-Japanese War, the Treaty of Shimonoseki was signed between China and Japan, with Li Hongzhang representing China's Qing government, and Ito Hirobumi on the Japanese side. Under the treaty, China would recognize Japanese authority over Korea; cede to Japan the Liaodong Peninsula, Taiwan (with its attached islets), and the Pescadores Islands; pay an indemnity of 200,000,000 taels of silver to Japan; open new trade ports and permit Japanese merchants to trade freely. The humiliating Treaty of Shimonoseki further pushed China into a semi-colonial state, arousing growing nationalism among the Chinese people.

● In 1894 (year of Jiawu in the lunar calendar), Japanese armies invaded Korea and China, but met with strong resistance in China, triggering the Sino-Japanese war. Soon, the Korean Peninsula fell under Japanese occupation. At sea, the Japanese navy gained maritime command after it defeated the Beiyang Navy of China. The Japanese advanced to attack northeast China on land and the coastal cities of Shandong Province from the sea, annihilating the Beiyang Navy. After the defeat, China was forced to sign the Treaty of Shimonoseki.

The negotiation meeting of the
"Treaty of Shimonoseki"

© 1895: German physicist Wilhelm Conrad Röntgen (1845-1923) produced and detected the x-ray.

Yuan Shikai

Yuan Shikai

Yuan Shikai (1859-1916), was the leader of the Beiyang Army. In 1895, he was recommended by Li Hongzhang to train the New Army in Tianjin. As commander-in-chief, he quickly raised his own troops. In the Hundred Days' Reform of 1898, Yuan gave the reformists away to win support from the Qing court. The next year, his successful suppression of the Boxer Movement won him a name in China and abroad. Yuan's official career was suspended briefly, for the Manchurian nobles felt threatened by his powerful Beiyang Army. Shortly after the Xinhai Revolution of 1911, Yuan was restored to the post with the hope that he would help the Qing court. However, Yuan joined the revolutionary side and forced the Qing emperor to abdicate. In 1912, Yuan became the provisional president of the Republic of China, and took office as president the following year. In 1915, Yuan proclaimed himself "Emperor," in an attempt to revive the monarchy. However, the next year he was forced to abandon monarchism under nationwide condemnation. He died in Beijing shortly after.

Zhang Jian

Nantong Museum (founded by Zhang Jian), the first Chinese-established museum

Zhang Jian (1853-1926), born in Nantong, Jiangsu Province, was a capitalist and constitutionalist in modern China. At the age of 41, he gained first place in the imperial examinations. Instead of pursuing a post in the court, Zhang devoted himself to industry and education. In 1895, he set up the Dasheng Cotton Mill in Nantong, and created the Dasheng Group with the establishment of the Huaihai Bank. As a scholar, Zhang's concern over education urged him to set up the Tongzhou Normal School, Tongzhou Girls' Normal School, and over 10 vocational schools. Zhang also sponsored libraries and museums. In the constitutional movement of the late Qing, Zhang united civil representatives of local provinces to present a petition in Beijing demanding the establishment of a national assembly.

► Yan Fu and *Evolution and Ethics*

► Late Qing satirical novels

► The Metropolitan University

► Yan Fu (1854-1921) was an accomplished scholar and translator. From 1877 to 1879, Yan studied in England, and upon graduation returned to China to teach. Roused after the First Sino-Japanese War, Yan took up the pen to condemn feudal autocracy and intractable conservatives, advocating learning from Western countries to save China. As a translator, Yan translated Thomas Huxley's *Evolution and Ethics*, as *Tianyanlun*, and introduced Darwin's theory of "natural selection" to Chinese readers.

► The late 19th century was a period when disillusionment towards the Qing government spread among the Chinese people. Literature at this time generally reflected and criticized social reality, referred to as the "late Qing satirical novels." Among these novels, four have enjoyed an enduring reputation: *Revealing Original Forms in Officialdom* by Li Baojia (1867-1906), *Odd Things Witnessed over Twenty Years* by Wu Jianren (1866-1910), *The Travels of Lao Can* by Liu E (1857-1909), and *A Flower in the Sea of Sins* by Zeng Pu (1872-1935).

► The Metropolitan University, predecessor of Peking University, was opened in 1898 as the first university in modern China. With the aim of "cultivating pragmatic professionals," the school board planned to set up departments of natural science, politics, agriculture, industry, and commerce. More departments were set up by the year 1910, including departments of economics, law, arts, sciences, agriculture, industry, and commerce. In 1912, the school was renamed, "Peking University."

Yan Fu and a facsimile of *Evolution and Ethics*

Present-day west gate of Peking University

© 1897: Italian inventor Guglielmo Marconi (1874-1937) developed wireless telegraphy.

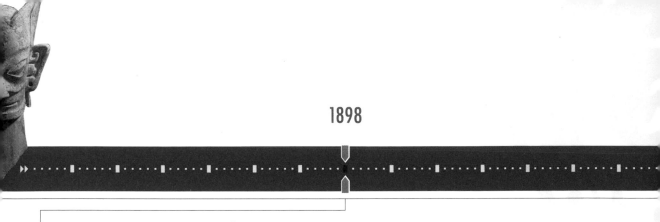

The Hundred Days' Reform   The Boxer Movement (1898-1900)

Tan Sitong, who was killed in the coup after the Hundred Days' Reform

In response to China's defeat in the First Sino-Japanese War, a petition was presented to the young Emperor Guangxu (r. 1875-1908) by 1,300 students led by Kang Youwei, demanding a new political system of constitutional monarchy to "seek prosperity through reforms." Beginning in June 1898, Emperor Guangxu ordered a series of sweeping political, economic, cultural and military reforms. However, the 103-day reform was ended by a coup engineered by the conservative Empress Dowager Cixi, forcing Emperor Guangxu into seclusion, and removing reform-minded officials from office.

The Boxer (Righteous Harmony Society) was the secret martial arts society active in northern China, which launched the Boxer Movement in 1898, sweeping across Shandong, Hebei, Beijing, Tianjin, and all across northeastern China. The movement upheld the slogan, "Support the Qing to annihilate the foreigners." The movement was actually used as a tool against the foreigners by the Qing government, who in turn feared the power of the Boxers. Demands from Westerners were placed upon the Qing court to quash the movement, and the short-lived society was ended thereafter.

A flag of the Boxers: "Support the Qing; destroy the foreigners"

© 1898: Polish physicist Marie Curie (1867-1934) discovered the radioactive element Radium.

Kang Youwei

Liang Qichao

A native of Nanhai, Guangdong Province, Kang Youwei (1858-1927) was initially a student of classical Confucianism, who in 1879 began to seek

Kang Youwei

political reforms through the integration of Western philosophies into a Chinese framework. Advocating reform and constitutional monarchy in the name of Confucianism, in 1891 Kang published *On the False Classics of Hsin Learning* and *On the Reform Theory of Confucius*. During the period from 1895 to 1898, Kang initiated the *Wan Guo Gong Bao* (*Review of the Times*), Qiangxuehui (Society for National Strengthening), and Baoguohui (Defend China Society). To urge Emperor Guangxu into action, Kang petitioned four times, before successfully persuading the emperor to adopt reform measures. After the failure of the reform, Kang fled abroad, continuing his cause of constitutional monarchy and remaining opposed to republicanism. In his old age, Kang devoted himself to education and writing, producing abundant intellectual works.

A student of Kang Youwei, Liang Qichao (1873-1929) was a co-leader with Kang in the Hundred Days' Reform of 1898. As editor-in-chief of a newspaper in Shanghai, Liang advocated the necessity for reform, exerting significant social influence. After the failure of the reform, Liang fled to Japan, continuing his advocacy of constitutional monarchy, before his return to China in 1913. As a prominent scholar with profound knowledge in Chinese and Western studies, Liang was highly accomplished in the areas of literature, history, philosophy, and Buddhism.

Liang Qichao and *Current Affairs*, a newspaper he founded

The Eight-Nation Alliance invaded China

The Boxer Protocol

The Eight-Nation Alliance troops landing at Dagu, Tianjin

The Eight-Nation Alliance was a coalition of the United Kingdom, the United States, Germany, France, Russia, Japan, Italy, and Austria-Hungary. The coalition army first attacked the Dagu Forts and occupied Tianjin, on the pretext that the Qing government had encouraged the Boxers to kill foreigners. Then they advanced to occupy the capital Beijing, looting and burning the city and the imperial gardens of the Old Summer Palace. The Qing royal family fled to Xi'an, and Li Hongzhang was left in Beijing to negotiate a treaty with the representatives of the eight powers and of Spain, Belgium and the Netherlands, who also wanted a share. After the signing of the humiliating "Boxer Protocol," the alliance armies pulled out of Beijing.

Signed in 1901, the "Boxer Protocol" was an unequal treaty between the Qing government and the 11 Western powers. According to the protocol, the Qing government had to punish those officials involved in the Boxer Movement, pay an indemnity of 450 million taels of silver, allow foreign countries to base troops in the legation quarters, destroy the Dagu Forts, allow foreign military deployment along the railway from Beijing to Shanhaiguan, and forbid Chinese people to found or join any anti-Western organizations. Chinese sovereignty was severely infringed upon under the Boxer Protocol, with foreign hold over China further consolidated.

Negotiation meeting for the Boxer Protocol

Zhang Binglin

Chen Tianhua

Zhang Binglin

Zhang Binglin (1869-1936), courtesy name Taiyan, was initially a pro-reformist, who later advocated complete revolution, countering the reform movement. After the 1911 Revolution, Zhang returned to China from Japan, to try to fulfill his political convictions. Utterly against the New Culture Movement, Zhang advocated "reverence for Confucianism and study of the classics," and opened a school in Suzhou in 1935 to preach Confucianism. A prominent scholar, Zhang was an accomplished figure in philosophy, literature, history, and linguistics. For his profound understanding of Chinese classics, Zhang has been acknowledged by later generations as a "Master of Sinology."

Chen Tianhua (1875-1905) was a democratic revolutionary and activist in modern China. He used simple language to publicize democratic revolution in his works, such as *Soul-Searching* and *Alarm Bells*, playing a significant role in the overthrow of the Qing Dynasty. In 1905, Chen took part in the drafting of *Principles of Revolution*, the platform of the Tongmenghui (Chinese United League). Later in December, in protest against the Japanese government deportation of Chinese students, Chen drowned himself in a Tokyo bay, leaving behind his *Last Testament* to inspire all Chinese overseas students.

Facsimiles of *Alarm Bells* and *Soul-Searching*

© 1903: At its 2ⁿᵈ Congress, the Russian Social Democratic Labor Party (RSDLP) split into Bolsheviks and Mensheviks. The emergence of Bolshevism marked the birth of Leninism.

201

Zou Rong

Zou Rong

Zou Rong (1885-1905) was a revolutionary theorist in modern China, who studied in Japan at the young age of 17. Upon his return to Shanghai in 1903, Zou published *Revolutionary Army*, a book advocating the overthrow of the Qing regime and the establishment of a republic. Fearing its influence, the Qing government jailed Zou. Two years later Zou died in prison.

Facsimile of the *Revolution Army*

Qiu Jin

Qiu Jin (1879-1907) was a revolutionary martyr in modern China. In 1904, Qiu went to study in Japan, where she participated in the revolutionary activities of Chinese overseas students. The next year, Qiu joined the Restoration Society and the Chinese United League. Qiu returned to China in 1906, protesting against the Japanese government's expulsion of Chinese students. In 1907, she gathered a military force to plot an uprising against the Qing government. After the uprising failed, Qiu Jin was arrested and executed.

Qiu Jin

End of the Imperial Examination System

An examination hall in Guangzhou in the late Qing

In the 1898 Hundred Days' Reform, Emperor Guangxu replaced the writing of the "Eight-Legged Essay" with policy writing, as an improvement to the Imperial Examination System. This examination system, having lasted for over 1,300 years, was finally abolished in 1905. After its abolition, graduates from new schools and foreign universities began to occupy an increasing number of posts in the government, and the education system in China entered a modern phase in a real sense.

● **Tongmenghui (Chinese United League)**
● **Zhan Tianyou and the construction of the Beijing-Zhangjiakou Railway (1905-1909)**

● The Chinese United League was established through the unification of several revolutionary organizations under a proposal by Sun Yat-sen in 1905. With common goals to overthrow the Qing regime and to establish a republic, the organizations came together as one in Tokyo, Japan, with the platform: "To overthrow the Manchu empire and to restore China to the Chinese, to establish a republic, and to distribute land equally among the people." The revolutionaries also drafted the Constitution of Tongmenghui, and Principles of Revolution. Branches were set up in China and abroad to undertake the cause. In 1911, the headquarters of the Chinese United League were relocated to Shanghai, and later to Nanjing, where the organization was restructured into the Kuomintang (Nationalist Party) in 1912.

Photo of Sun Yat-sen and members of the
Chinese United League in Singapore

Zhan Tianyou

● A native of Nanhai, Guangdong Province, Zhan Tianyou (Jeme Tien Yow, 1861-1919) was sent to the US for education in 1872, where he majored in Civil Engineering, with a focus on railroad construction, at Yale University. Upon graduation in 1881, Zhan returned to China. During the period from 1905 to 1909, Zhan, as Chief Engineer, built the Beijing-Zhangjiakou (Peking-Kalgan) Railway, the first self-financing railroad constructed without foreign assistance. Zhan adopted a zigzag design to overcome steep gradients, and the construction was completed two years ahead of schedule under a budget about 70 percent less than that estimated by foreigners.

The opening ceremony of the
Imperial Peking-Kalgan Railway

○ 1905-1907: Russian Revolution of 1905, a failed bourgeois democratic revolution in Russia.

○ 1907: The Anglo-Russian Entente, along with the Entente Cordiale (1904) and the Franco-Russian Alliance (1892), formed the Triple Entente between the UK, France and Russia, marking the formation of two great power groups in Europe.

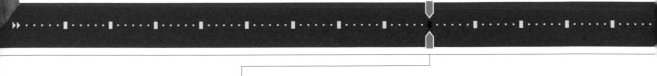

● Puyi, last emperor of the Qing Dynasty

● Puyi (1906-1967) was the last emperor of the Qing Dynasty. Enthroned in 1908, he ruled as Emperor Xuantong until his abdication in February 1912. In October 1924, he was overthrown and expelled from Beijing's Forbidden City. In 1932, Puyi was installed by the Japanese as the puppet ruler in occupied northeast China, and two years later was proclaimed "Emperor of Manchukuo." In 1959, Puyi began working as a researcher in Chinese history and literature. In 1967, he died of illness in Beijing. Puyi wrote an autobiography, *The First Half of My Life — from Emperor to Citizen*.

Puyi

● The Xinhai Revolution (Chinese Revolution of 1911)

The First National Assembly of the Republic of China

● From the early 20th century, revolutionary ideas and organizations sprouted around China. In such circumstances, it was not surprising to see a nationwide protest against the Qing government's transfer of railway construction rights to foreign hands, which served as a trigger for a complete revolution. On October 10, the Wuchang Uprising broke out, followed by independence declared by over 10 provinces. The Qing Dynasty soon disintegrated. On January 1, 1912, the interim government of the Republic of China was founded in Nanjing, with Sun Yat-sen as the provisional president. On February 12, the abdication of Emperor Puyi marked the end of the 2,000-year feudal autocracy in China. The 1911 Revolution is alternatively called the "Xinhai Revolution," since it occurred in the Chinese lunar calendar's Xinhai year.

© 1910: Korea was forced to sign the Japan-Korea Annexation Treaty, under which Japan annexed Korea, starting the period of Japanese rule.

INDEX

NAMES AND PLACES

HISTORICAL EVENTS

CULTURE
AND TECHNOLOGY

图书在版编目（CIP）数据

中国历史速查：英文 /《中国历史速查》编写组编著．
北京：外文出版社，2008
ISBN 978-7-119-05487-2
Ⅰ．中... Ⅱ．中... Ⅲ．中国—历史—工具书—英文　Ⅳ．K20-6

中国版本图书馆 CIP 数据核字（2008）第 146230 号

策　　划：周明伟　李振国
出版指导：李振国　胡开敏

英文翻译：徐汀汀　章挺权　欧阳伟萍
英文审定：May Yee　汪光强
中文审定：萧师铃
责任编辑：杨春燕　李建安　刘芳念
装帧设计：黎　红
印刷监制：张国祥

本书的出版得到张侃、国务院新闻办公室图片库等的帮助，特此鸣谢。

中国历史速查

本书编写组　编著

© 2008 外文出版社

出版发行：

外文出版社（中国北京百万庄大街 24 号）
邮政编码：100037
网　　址：www. flp. com. cn
电　　话：008610 - 68320579（总编室）
　　　　　008610 - 68995852（发行部）
　　　　　008610 - 68327750（版权部）
制　　版：北京维诺传媒文化有限公司
印　　制：外文印刷厂
开　　本：787mm×1092mm　1/16
印　　张：16
2008 年第 1 版第 1 次印刷
（英）
ISBN 978-7-119-05487-2
11000（平）
17-E-6829 P

LDF
2010